INCOME-BASED REPRESENTATION

Jordan David Weisinger, M.S., M.P.P.A., M.B.A.

ACKNOWLEDGMENTS

This book is nearly identical to another title written by Jordan Weisinger titled "Democratic-Socialism". Only the forward and first chapter are different. The material for this book was also used in another printing titled "The Fury; Class Struggles and Income-based Representation". Two prior versions of this book were discontinued. The names of the books were "Class Struggles" and "Market Democracy".

This book is an abbreviated version of other books by Jordan David Weisinger titled "GDP-based Representation" (2018) and "The Fountain; Nation Building with Econometric Representation" (2018). All material in this book was resourced from the original book.

1. "Provisional Democracy   describes provisional (emergency) governments during wars of succession or secession.

2. "Public   Policy-based   Protests: Resistance Strategies   for   Mayors,   Governors,   and Legislators" describes strategic nonviolent protest strategies like tax embargoes, default, shutdowns, and economic sanctions.

3. "Insurrection: Essays on Institutional Protests and Regime Change" describes indicators of growing authoritarian parties and public policy to reform back to democracy.

4. "Asset-based   Representation   describes econometric representation based on home ownership, with strong anti-discriminatory properties.

5. "Tax-based Representation describes econometric representation based on tax liabilities, with modest anti-discriminatory properties.

6. "GDP-based Representation (aka Imperial Democracy)" describes econometric representation based on GDP, with modest anti-discriminatory and imperial properties.

Table of Contents

FOREWARD

Biological organisms are in a constant struggle of survival. They will either outperform their environment or succumb to it. The more quickly they evolve to overcome their environment, the more quickly their environment changes to match or exceed their capabilities. States and nations are, in essence, no different than other organisms. They are like the titans of the Greek mythology, with a thousand arms and a thousand eyes, looking to overcome every obstacle in their path. Societies and economies are more capable than individuals but they are harder to control and direct. Nations either rely on the discretion of an authoritarian or on the whims of a half-educated electorate. Sates take nation security seriously, because every nation is in a tentative state. All of its weaknesses will be exploited. All of its missteps recorded. Often, nations are hunted by their enemies on the outside, and from dissidents or reformers from the inside. The more successful states can impose their will through law, trade, or partnership in a way similar to how biological organisms pass their traits onto their offspring. Generations learn from those that come before them, they live in the neighborhoods created by their ancestors, they abide by the laws passed by those coming before them.

Theories of evolutionary biology are description of risk. If a nation does not evolve constantly through public policy and immigration, it slows down and become more vulnerable. If the nation does not exhibit the political will to regulate industry and tax its own citizens, it will start to sink into the swamp of corruption and wealth inequality. If it passes to many restrictive laws and burdens its citizens with too many taxes, they will start to organize against the state. There is no single solution that delivers a viable and secure nation. It is a moving average, based on current conditions but always framed by the past. The electorates disappointment is proportional to the difference between expected outcomes and realized outcomes. When there is too large of a spread between the two outcomes, the electorate becomes susceptible to outside influences and more eradicate in their judgement. It is during these moments they can be moved by radicalism and manipulated by foreign interlopers.

Democracies are more susceptible to foreign interference than other nation. By their very nature, they are open to disinformation and misdirection. The civil liberties that protect them from illegal surveillance and grant them access to unvetted media sources, also makes them vulnerable to foreign powers sowing dissent and discord to destroy their society and government. There is no easy solution. More open societies are stronger and more durable, but predators usually target the people on the margins of society. They tailor their misinformation campaigns around prejudices, primordial fears, and historic grudges. Persons in the margins vote and they can have unpredictable effects on elections. They also organize and mobile into movements with counter-productive agendas. The disaffected and disenfranchised are more incentivized to take risks to change their deplorable lives. They have less to lose and more to gain. They also share scant incentivizes with the elites and establishments. In a crisis, these less conventional and less viable ideas may catch fire, as ordinary citizens succumb to the fear of job loss, death, or political disenfranchisement.

Organisms only evolve to satisfy the immediate demands of their environment. If their environment changes, thy may find themselves hunted, exploited, or oppressed. Organisms successful in ordinary situations may not be able to adapt quick enough to changes in climate, or scarcity of prey, or the inability to overcome natural boundaries. There is no organizational aim of evolution other than survival. Humans are no different. Societies that adapt to periods of abundance and security may not adjust quickly enough to new environments of climate change, wealth inequality, or immigration and demographic shifts. When their expectations are not met, they will become confused, angry, scared, and susceptible to dangerous new ideologies. The need to overcome some immediate threat will coerce support for failed ideas like fascism or communism. Democracy must respond by evolving itself. It has to accommodate the defects of capitalist economy, before scarcity and corruption can be exploited by authoritarian parties for their own benefit. If structural reforms in the legislatures can help inoculate the nation from demagogues seeking to exploit inequality, moderates will accept it as the best solution to the risk of fascism. If moderates wish to preserve their equity in the market economy and their influence in the political markets, they will accept the improved role identity and class division of the electorate.

The median partition is like a vaccine. It is immunization against wealth inequality and discrimination. It injects role identity and partisan class rhetoric into the political process, moving the electorate to vote more in their own interests. It reduces the opportunities foreign nations and radicals have to disrupt civil society and the democratic process. When the public hears and sees more violent and extreme rhetoric, it can digest it as less productive and more dangerous. The language of division will be less effective because most of the issues will entrenched within conventional politics. When the electorate is more able to debate and act on inequality through public policy, the need for more extreme solutions like communism and authoritarianism produce less urgency and necessity. The body-politic won't over-react to crises, because they are more certain they can overcome them with debate and public policy.

Democratic-socialism is the belief that socialist economic outcomes can be acquired through the democratic process. This is contradictory in the sense that a democratic society will impose centrally controlled economy on themselves with no deviation or recourse. Communism was an outgrowth from the political reality that socialism could never be achieved in conventional democracies. Communism demanded a violent overthrow of government by the proletariat so they could impose centrally controlled economy on their own citizens. Communism was an abject failure for this reason. In contemporary democracies, the presence of competitive political markets will ensure that any movements toward socialist outcomes will be tempered by movements bent on privatization or market-based solutions. Today, Democratic-socialism is the endeavor to impose strong regulations on the industry has competitive markets while striving to distribute high quality government benefits when inflexible commodities like healthcare and education are concerned.

Democratic-Socialism is the attitude or belief that a people can make decisions about compensation, taxes, and benefits in the same capacity a firm owner sets wages and expectations for their employees. Governments are intended to intervene where unions fail. Governments are the only recourse to firms and owners seeking to pay the lowest amount for wages and taxes, and the highest amount for commodities and services, while preserving near monopolistic control over markets. Democratic-Socialism is the expectation that competitive political markets with balances representational systems will produced mixed market outcomes that elevate individuals and families above firms, while continuing to support market-based solutions for the lion's share of the economy.

Attitude is not enough to get a nation from where it is to where it should be. The current iteration of Democratic-Socialism is primarily a belief system that remains unsupported by balanced and accurate systems of representation. If Democratic-Socialism is to achieve its stated goals, it must advocate for permanent changes the architecture of government. In order for socialism to remain relevant and viable, it must remake itself in the image of democracy. The best way it can do this is by imposing a median partition on a demographic-based legislature. The median partition splits the electorate into two equally sized population based on median income. Exactly half the population will have an income of zero or less than the median income and vote in the lower chamber. Exactly half of the population will have above median incomes and vote in the upper chamber. When the below median income earners are segregated in the lower chamber, they are given a classed identity, charged with purpose and aligned by shared economic interests. The below median chamber is in most aspects, equivalent to the proletariat described by socialism. Instead of achieving socialism through violence, the proletariat will participate in the democratic process and pursue their interest through public policy and reform. Their unique identity and interest will ensure the economy works for their benefit, in addition to the whims and expectations of the firm owners and leisure class.

Without the median partition, Democratic-Socialists can't guarantee the interests of the under-class and working class over the history of a nation. Political parties come in and out of favor depending on the success of their policies. In order for the public to gauge the effectiveness of those policies, they must first be passed. If the Democratic-Socialists find themselves in a nation with irregularly organized institutions, weak voter turnout, and easily obstructed legislatures, they will quickly lose favor with the public as they won't be able to support their promises with outcomes. The strength of the Democratic-Socialist message is predicated on actually acquiring laws that control wealth inequality, ameliorate poverty, protect voting rights and civil rights. If the Democratic-Socialist can deliver on their promises, they won't have any credibility and won't win many elections. This is why Democratic-Socialism must become synonymous with the median partition. The movement must be remade into the party of Market Democrats. The median partition makes it far more likely that the nation passes the reforms necessary to maintain a well-regulated and equality economy. The median is the only permanent reform the Democratic-Socialist can acquire that makes it much more likely they acquire all of their other stated goals.

One of the most important properties discussed in Capitalism is the creation of value from the division of labor. When workers specialize their labor, they can improve the rate of production and the quality of production, increasing the revenues earned by their combined effort. The example used is pin production. Pins aren't overly complex products to manufacture but there are several distinct steps. It may take any single individual an hour to produce 2 pins if they are responsible for every phase of production. When the phases of production are split between individuals each responsible for a single part, 10 labors might produce 30 pins. Individually the 10 laborers might produce 20 pins but when they specialize, they could produce 50% more pins. Not only, will the group produce more pins, but the pins will likely be higher quality when each laborer perfects their specific role within production. This is the value created by the division and specialization of labor.

This concept can be applied to political markets when the electorate is split by the median income value into two more specialized parts. Each of the classed electorates will work harder to pass laws that more directly benefit their shared interests. The below median electorate will enthusiastically pursue higher minimum wages, stronger union and labor laws, and more progressive taxes. The below median chamber becomes specialized at identifying and supporting policies that increase equity and opportunity in the generalized economy. This isn't always achievable in contemporary democracies. The lower classes confuse their interests with the owner's classes and leisure classes and the quality of legislative production suffers. When the proletariat is isolated within the below median chamber, they will acquire that role identity and organize more effectively to protect their interests. The below median electorate will be able to develop the bureaucracy and infrastructure needed to successfully craft and enforce laws favoring their class identity.

The nation gains value from this specialization of interests. When the electorate is undifferentiated, its laws only reflect the interest of the median voter or the owners class. The workers and citizens on the margins are often ignored. This empowers the most vulnerable parts of society to be responsible themselves rather than patiently waiting for others to pass laws accommodating for market deficiencies. In conventional democracies, the political caste is often far richer than the rest of the population. They have fixed wages more than two times the median wage and ten times the minimum wage. They may occasionally pursue policies that favor the underclass and lower class, but it is at a distance, viewed as guardianship rather than individual benefit. The representatives of the below median chamber will have similar incomes as their constituencies, making them fare better advocates. They will pursue policies that directly benefit the below median income group because they are only paid a median wage.

The nation also gains value from increased competition in the political markets. When the electorate is split into two, it makes the political parties more competitive by forcing them to win offices in both chambers. A political platform that does well in one chamber is not guaranteed to do well in the other. This is not an obstacle in most conventional democracies whose undifferentiated chambers are often dominated by parties with single perspective platforms. A political party will have to adapt policies that can pass the below median chamber as well as the above median chamber. Parties are evaluated in terms of the laws they pass, not the laws they support. If the party isn't competitive, it will be viewed as weak or ineffective and not attract the support it needs to continue as a national party. The need to produce legislative outcomes, will result in more incremental reforms and higher-quality laws, producing value for constituents in both chambers.

Income-based Representation is the inevitable result of failures in conventional democracies to deliver on high quality democratic entitlements and civil rights for their citizenry and residence. It is very similar to the premise of Democratic Socialism but Democratic Socialism differs from Income-based Representation in that the tenants of socialism are captured by the machinery of the democratic process rather than the imposition of centrally managed economies. It should not be confused with the radical ideology of Communism. Das Kapital and the Communist Manifesto demanded the proletariat take control of the government and drastically redistribute wealth and destroy the institutions of mercantile economy. Income-based Representation does not advocate for such extreme measures or outcomes, but rather elevates the below median income group by separating them from the above median income group, providing them the representation they need to reform the economy, protect their civil rights and their voting rights. The proletariat is made a partner rather than a master, and through the enhanced democratic process, a more equitable and just economy will be earned. Certain industries must be centrally managed but most perform much better through markets and free trade.

Income-based Representation advocates for high quality democratic entitlements that protect majority rule with strong checks and balances within government institutions. It is the expectation that the division of labor in representation produce more value for the nation when its public policy benefits from the increased expertise through role identity, and the compartmentalization of interests through the median partition. All of the stakeholders can pursue their individual interests, with the product being more equitable markets, more specialized public policy, and more accurate and honest elections. Income-based Representation has properties that enhances the representation for discriminated minorities and poorer populations making it the best choice for nation-building and reform movements. If the citizens are more informed and given the choice between conventional democracy and Income-based Representation, they will invariably choose the system that better advocates for their civil rights and economic rights.

History teaches hard lessons. If the failures of capitalism are not corrected through the democratic process, the threat of radical ideologies will resurface as support for authoritarianism gains traction in the margins of society. Demagogues and organizations will exploit every opportunity for profit and personal political power. When the public is hungry and fearful, they will hold onto any belief system that promises food and shelter This is the most dangerous period for a nation and democratic nations are more susceptible. In democracy, the hungry, the cold, and the scared vote.

However, most of the inherent defects of capitalism can be cured through public policy and the democratic process. Market economy is not perfect and nobody expects all demand to be satisfied by incentives and price points. These deficiencies can be corrected by public policy and economic engineering. If all persons are equally represented in the political market, it maximizes the probability of the electorate arriving as the most appropriate and equitable solution. Electorates are self-correcting. When they over regulate in one decade, they will pursue deregulation the following decade. Political markets constantly re-evaluate their own price points according to changing demand functions.

When the classes are split by the median, each electorate acquires role identity and this will help them understand the public policy from their own perspective. Wage constraints on the below median income chamber will align the interests of the voters with their representatives. Each representative will view the bills voted on in terms of how they impact their current financial position. This improves agency within the political system. The properties of role identity and improved agency will contribute to more frequent and more productive economic reforms being passed through the legislature. Only class-based representation provides the electorate the specialized representation it needs to overcome the reoccurring deficiencies of market economy while avoiding the pitfalls of socialism.

Class-based representation is the most rational and appropriate responses to the failures of market economy. Splitting the electorate by class and then setting them into opposition will produce the public policy necessary to correct the deficiencies in capitalism. Nonviolence is the best defense against exploitation and oppression when accompanied with public debate and due process. The median voter will decide the outcome of most elections and their experiences will dominate their candidate and policy choices. When deficiencies exist in compensation, working conditions, taxes, or government benefits, they will respond by voting for the party or candidates that support policies that correct those deficiencies. Only more accurate and honest representation will allow a nation to respond with the appropriate market responses and avoid the dangers of rebellion and revolt.

When rebel states surrender, they may be repatriated back into the union, but they must not be allowed to immediately resume their former position and status as the dominant opposition party without any structural changes to the political process. The establishment party can take their chances by using naturalization of immigrant enlisted and emancipated city-states, but the better strategy is to coerce the state into making changes to their own constitutions, which will disrupt the rebel party's monopoly on state-level elections. Many of the econometric variables available provide substantial anti-discriminatory properties, making them the perfect reform to perpetually disrupt and ethno-authoritarian party's ability to organize another coup or secession.

Occupied nations are generally converted to democracy after conflict to promote civil liberties and economic growth making future conflict less likely, but when the offending states are already democratic, the political disposition of its institutions must be altered to change the trajectory of public policy back towards peace and prosperity. Econometric representation is a tool useful to occupying or expansionary democracies, that allow democracies to intervene in other democracies, without reverting to lower-quality authoritarian systems of control, while making permanent and lawful changes that disrupt the regime empowering the belligerent political parties.

There are two pathways to econometric occupation after conflict. When rebel states take up arms against a democratic nation, they can be forcibly put down and repatriated. When the state surrenders its arms, the current administration can be threatened with incarceration or worse sanctions, with the intent to make permanent changes to the state constitution before new elections produce a more productive and loyal administration. The first pathway introduces substantial risk with unpredictable outcomes associated with the use of violence, resource allocation, and outside influence. The second pathway avoids the upfront risk of violence and displaces it across a longer period of time but where non-violent economic and trade interventions increase the odds of success.

The repatriation process is much more complicated when rebel states are permitted to peaceably secede from the union, but it may be the more conservative, more effective, and more productive method for coercing the wayward states back into the Union. An establishment party can rely on trade embargoes, economic sanctions, privateering laws, and a whole suite of strategic nonviolent methods to break the public finance systems and make the economy so unprofitable, that a substantial portion of the public and firms within the states will seek repatriation. Prior to readmission, the state can be forced to make permanent changes to their constitution, ensuring all the long-term goals of the establishment party and democratic government can be achieved through peaceful reform. The second, slower but nonviolent method should preserve the most lives, enlisted and civilian, with the threat of military intervention available in most scenarios if the public is being subjugated with mass murder and incarceration, which may result in future homicides in economies of scale.

In the United States, a democratic federal government could leverage tax embargoes from its allied states, which control 57% of the GDP, to withhold the federal tax subsidies that provides 20% of GOP state revenues to fund operations, with the explicit intent to coerce Confederate states, which had been permitted to successfully secede, back into the union using economic sanctions alone. With the democratic allies in office, they could easily organize city-wide tax embargoes on Confederate states, cutting them off from 70-80% of GDP and another 40-60% of their annual tax subsidies.

Not only would the Confederate states not have enough money to field their grossly over-weighted National Guard Armies, but their states would also be in default status, not being able to cover ordinary expenses and losing access to deficit financing after New York City cuts them off from the bond markets with tax penalties and financial regulations. Even without resorting to violence, a democratic federal government and participating states could coerce the Confederate states back into the Union, individually when separated from the group, and only after they agree to terms found suitable to the state leadership and current federal elected legislature and executive.

If the democratic party can emancipate a substantial proportion of cities within the rebel states, while preserving the lions' share of GDP from the original union, it will reduce the incentives for rebel leadership to successfully secede. The wealth of nations is found within its cities, and most of the economic activity of the nation is found on its coasts. Even if the rebels successfully secede, they could be reduced to just 10-20% of their former economic and military power, when compared to their former position as dominant political party in the combined nation. When the GOP is reduced to a poor rural nation, they will be much more susceptible to repatriation through trade embargoes and privateering efforts, when the sanctions persist after independence is gained.

It could take several years, but every election cycle will pose a risk to a Republican regime, with more and more of the voters wanting to re-establish normal relation with their former sovereign and fellow states. Even in an authoritarian environment, firm owners and the wealthiest families will desperately want to promote trade and tourism between the states and the new economic or political unions. The longer the rebel states remain separated, the worse the economic conditions will get or the bigger the wealth gap between the new confederate republic and democratic establishment states will grow.

During negotiations of surrender or repatriation, there is enough variety in econometric variables to accommodate a wide variety of interests, cultural preferences, political agendas or ideologies while arresting most concerns of the occupying democratic powers. Not all risk can be eliminated for all parties but enough of the short-term threats can be mitigated to give the new arrangement enough confidence to survive long enough for new generations to adopt new cultures and form new expectations based on new probabilities and new opportunities. One of the biggest advantages is that the occupying power can offer the surrendering state governments options for choosing the representational coefficients and number of institutions, so they have some agency in choosing the new structure for their state governments. The establishment party can tailor the options offered to meet their own need, but the Confederates will have some input into which econometric variables are used, knowing they will shape future electorates and culture.

The regional governments formed earlier to finance and prosecute the war will have their own representational coefficients, which may be econometric with their own anti-discriminatory properties and influence on the culture. When regional governments are available, it creates more flexibility when selecting the state econometric representational coefficients, simply because the power of the state will be already be subrogated and far less likely to organize into a subsequent rebellion. By the time the state is repatriated, the political disposition of the entire nation may already have substantially changed by emancipated city-states, naturalized immigrant enlisted, amendments changing the composition of the courts or changing Senators to districts rather than state-wide jurisdictions, so there will be less emphasis on changing the state-level constitutions or institutions but any neglect during the occupation could be unforgiveable by future generations if it is exploited for war.

Each of the major econometric representational coefficients provides different utilities when they are applied to different state constitutions and regional governments. Generally, there is a straight method for distributing representational coefficients and another method relying on a median partition for each econometric variable considered for the occupation, reorganization, or repatriation. A straight method tallies the values of each economic variable between the states of a nation, or counties within a state, and allocates representatives to the chamber determined by the variable chosen for the calculation. The straight method isn't intended to be equitable or fair, instead being used as countervailing force to some other inequitable distribution of political power within the union. For example, if an institution like a Senate favors rural and poor states over wealthier and more populated states, a good remedy is to create a third chamber that over-represents the states being exploited or under-represented by the Senate.

A median chamber splits the electorate into two equal parts, separated by a median threshold determined by the econometric variable chosen. The number of seats allocated to the two median chambers can be proportional to population or some other representational coefficient, but the median partition will ensure the electorate will be split equally between the two chambers even if the coefficient is not proportional to population. Median thresholds are the best vector for equitable representation, with universal suffrage conserved between the two chambers, especially when the special properties of certain econometric variable produce strong anti-discriminatory properties in the electorate, changing the character or substance of the culture, making future rebellions far less likely or successful, when attempted, again, and again, if the hard lessons aren't learned by all parties.

The four most appropriate econometric coefficients for occupation or reconstruction are GDP, Income, Asset (Ownership), and Tax-based representation. There are many others, like debt and employment-based representation, with their own utilities and dependencies on data collection. Each term has distinct advantages which will be preferred by the occupying power or the occupied state. Even when the benefit isn't immediately obvious, making substantial changes to the power structure by introducing econometric representation on the state-level, will produce enough variability in future electoral outcomes to justify the acceptance by both the occupying and occupied states. However, when there is a clear cultural preference for prejudice and systemic racism, the occupying states must insist on a coefficient that empowers minorities, women, and the poor to maximize the opportunities for these groups to achieve reforms, permanently disrupting the systemic racism in institutions producing the ethno-authoritarian culture.

To illustrate the anti-discriminatory properties of econometric representation, a median partition based on income in the United States would divide the electorate into two equal parts, with the below median income earners in the lower chamber and the above median income earner in the upper chamber. When median income is examined through the prism of race and ethnicity, a larger number of African Americans. Hispanics, Native Americans, and other minority groups find themselves located in the lower chamber, giving the plurality a greater chance of earning a majority. If a single minority group has even just 26% of seats in a single chamber, they can effectively gain majority control of that chamber, if competitive elections split the chamber near equally between parties. A demographic group as small as just 13% of the overall population, could gain 26% and majority control over the lower chamber, if 100% of the population had below median incomes.

When discrimination is present in an economy, a larger portion of a minority group is bound to land in the below median chamber, making it more likely they use their influential position to boycott and filibuster the legislative process until the two chambers agree on civil rights and economic reforms that improve employment opportunities and wealth within the oppressed or exploited group. When the minority group acquires income equality and wealth parity, they will be more normally distributed amount the two chambers partitioned by median income, making the number of seats in one or both chambers more proportional to their population. Economic discrimination will produce enough political power to produce the necessary reforms to improve equality, bringing balance back to the allocation of seats among demographic groups in the state or nation. All the econometric variables have anti-discriminatory properties when minority demographic groups are treated differently from the majority demographic or each other. An econometric variable may have more of an impact on one demographic group than another at the time of incorporating the institutions, but this may change over time, especially with competitive elections.

When the democratic states form provisional governments that later convert into regional governments, there will likely be less resistance to econometric coefficients with anti-discriminatory properties. Most democratic states have the tendency to respect universal suffrage and prefer plurality, allowing them to use more progressive representational coefficients when they initially form the regions, so that repatriated states must conform to those terms in at least one tier of government after the conflict. Democratic provisional governments will need to pay special attention to attracting emancipated city-states, but they will likely accept the lowest-common denominator of demographic representation, allowing the establishment states to make more strategic decisions on the engineering solutions for their provisional governments.

When GDP is selected as the econometric variable, it is intended to give an advantage to wealthier states and counties, making it extremely useful for occupations and more permanent reorganizations. When wealthier and more populous states are over-represented in a GDP-based chamber, it offsets the arbitrary representation of a Senate. A Senate provides the same number of senators to each state regardless of population, making it an inverse to demographic representation, resembling more an aristocratic form of representation. Both GDP-based representation and an arbitrary-based coefficient may be considered aristocratic coefficients, one over-representing poor and rural states, while the other over-representing wealthier states, but more complex republican forms of government can use one to balance out the other, qualifying as democratic when universal suffrage remains enforced, but more reliable in unstable environments when the tension between the two chambers offset competing parties and regions.

GDP-based representation may deliver more seats to wealthier jurisdictions like cities, which tend to be heavily minority and poor, which has a short term anti-discriminatory property, but because cities are the fulcrum or locus of power, and cities are subject to markets like employment and housing, the resident beneficiaries may change over the long-term, making it more acceptable to all parties during the reorganization or occupation. While still residing within city boundaries, the minority groups can influence local political decisions, building more permanent urban multi-family housing, based on ownership, or make sure they aren't gentrified out of the neighborhood concentrating the GDP-representation for its residents.

One of the reasons early democracies were aristocratic is the natural inclination of the wealthy elite to protect the system that helped create their wealth and perpetuate it. Although exploitative, democracies are inherently unstable and vulnerable for the first few decades of incorporation. An aristocracy is more likely to resist dramatic reforms and protect the establishment, even when contemporary issues and institutions are split by parties. GDP-based representation has similar properties except it is more compatible with universal suffrage and unrestricted electorates. The wealthier states have a greater capacity to project their power and protect their political power, be it a democratic republic rather than an industrial aristocracy. A GDP-based system bestows a substantial amount of political influence in the cities and states with more economic power, placing it under democratic control, but otherwise creating incentives to protect the current paradigm and make incremental reforms towards more honest and accurate elections or more equitable economy.

When straight GDP-based representation is

imposed on state level institutions, it will concentrate a lions' share of political power within the cities. Urban populations are typically much more diverse than rural or even suburban populations, making it much more likely a substantial amount of political power is transferred to minorities, women, and young voters living within the districts of the city. Although the number of seats allocated to each state is derivate of GDP and economic influence, each one of those offices are democratically elected districts or jurisdictions. GDP-based coefficients still qualify as democratic-republican, which makes them one of the higher-quality forms of government that can be used in nation building.

If cities are giving majority power in just one of the two state legislative chambers through a GDP chamber, it will break up the trifectas an ethno-authoritarian party needs to wage a war of succession or secession. If just one of the bicameral chambers are changed into a straight GDP-based coefficient through the state legislature, it makes it very unlikely an ethno-authoritarian party will gain majorities in both chambers, eliminating the risk of subsequent rebellions. Of the 22 Confederate states most likely to have the trifectas needed within state governments to prosecute a war. Nine of those states see a concentration of GDP in democratically controlled cities that would produce majorities in at least one chamber. The states most susceptible to GDP-based occupation governments are Missouri with 96% of GDP located in democratically controlled cities, Utah with 53%, Indiana with 58%, Idaho with 54%, Louisiana with 72%, Tennessee with 79%, Texas with 65%, and Georgia with 84%. Many of the other rebel states would likely also find secure democratic majorities when all cities are tallied, as only the largest five cities in each state were considered.

The intended goal of an occupation and reorganization is to force the dominant demographic group to negotiate with minorities, women, and younger voters when they determine public policy, and placing at least one of the two state legislatures under firm control by urban districts with more diversity in age and demographics, makes it more likely public policy benefits all residents more equitably, while also ensuring the rebel states cant organize themselves again, when the opposition party can embargo all appropriations needed for war through control of the GDP-chamber. Utilizing GDP-based representation also at least partially satisfies the allies promises to emancipate city-states by giving them almost implicit and permanent control over one of the two legislative chambers of state government. The benefits aren't mutually exclusive with representation in the regional or federal governments, it's another opportunity. Cities that aid in the defense of the union could end up with majority control in a state legislature, reciprocal relationship in a regional government, and if emancipated with statehood, proportional representation in the federal government. Just one of these benefits may be worth the risk, especially when the consequence of inaction is authoritarianism.

Despite the anti-discriminatory properties of straight GDP-based representation, some of the Confederate leaders will prefer GDP-based coefficients because of the expansionary properties of the term. GDP-based representation allows states or cities to aggressively expand their border by treaty or war, when less wealthy states can be assimilated with very little chance future demographic changes produce undesirable changes resulting from the acquired satellite states. During conflict, many of the prior institutions and infrastructure of the occupied state will have been destroyed or dismantled, greatly reducing their current

GDP, making them more compatible with the occupying state even when democratic representation is guarantee. More conservative states may prefer straight GDP-based representation over other options because of the innate property of econometric representation. If they keep an eye to the future, GDP-based institutions on the federal or regional tiers of government may be the reform that produces the best outcomes for them, despite the electoral changes, because it utilizes their baser instincts to forward the interest of the nation.

The establishment party need not only impose GDP-based representation on individual states as they are repatriated. Instead, the establishment party could reorganize the regional government, emancipated states, or create a triangulation chamber by amendment. Predictably, a federal legislature predicated on straight GDP-based coefficients would produce a roughly 57%/43% advantage for Democrats if all states repatriated. Margins gets bigger if states successfully secede. Emancipated cities could raise this to roughly a 70%/30% advantage for Democrats, with similar advantages in Senate. No structural advantage would be permanent, with the Democratic party likely splitting between more conservative and liberal agendas, but the electorate will force the most conservative populations to adapt to the new environment and culture. Most rational nations are dominated by the more moderate candidates, especially when the average product of each party results in incremental reforms producing the median test for what qualifies as moderate. The 70/30% advantage should last long enough for the nation to move past a reconstruction period, avoiding subsequent threats of debt defaults, government shutdowns, and other insults that jeopardize the union.

A straight GDP coefficient is a blunt instrument

compared to its use in a median partition in either state or federal legislatures. A bicameral chamber premised on GDP-based representation splits the nation or state into two equal electorates, with each state or county separated into above-median GDP and below median GDP groups. Within a federal legislature, the states are separated into above and below median GDP groups. Within a state legislature, the counties are split into above median and below median GDP groups. The number of representatives allocated with the legislative chamber continues to be determined with a demographic coefficient, making it compatible with most contemporary higher-quality democratic regimes, but the regions of a nation may be broken apart, with neighboring states allocated to different chambers within the legislature. The wealthier states will be grouped in one chamber and the poorer states will be grouped in the other, irrespective of location, making it a classed system of representation, and an irreversible disruption to old cultures, traditions, and institutions.

Although, the political disposition of a federal institution will be predictably split down by conventional party lines, when it is applied to individual state legislatures, the median partition divides rural districts from city districts, allocating at least one chamber to the wealthier, more diverse, and more educated districts, possibly disrupting the ethno-authoritarian party from acquiring the trifectas they need to prosecute a coup or successfully seceding. Unlike straight GDP-based systems, representational coefficients are still determined by demographics, so the ethno-authoritarian party will likely maintain advantages in both legislative chambers, making it an inferior choice for occupation governments, but a superior choice for regional governments.

An income-based representation provides similar representation when used with straight coefficient, producing an institution where wealthier states or counties command a majority of seats. It has many of the same advantages for expansionary democracy or rewards for emancipated cities. The wealthier districts tend to be more urban, with more demographic diversity and more educated persons, which provides a benefit to more liberal parties. Income is highly derivative of GDP and the cities and states should have a similar political disposition as demonstrated in the GDP-based estimates. However, Income-based representation has discrete anti-discriminatory properties that are much more refined and predictable than GDP-based coefficients when used with a median partition.

When an electorate is split in two by a median income, the below median income earners are sent to one chamber and the above median income earners are sent to the other chamber. Politics is immediately and irrevocably intersected by class, which is normal, but the identities are more pronounced and clearly defined. Each class will enjoy majority control over one chamber, forcing the owners and investors class to negotiate labor and tax reforms with the working class and middle class, every single time they want to pass an annual budget, raise the debt ceiling, or distribute contracts and federal subsidies to their firms. Policy and rhetoric centered squarely on class will often be more unifying than anti-discriminatory language which always incites those who are either prejudiced or convinced they are race blind. Class-based rhetoric helps all working- and middle-class families, and even if it helps disadvantaged and discriminated against groups more, allowing it to unify the below median group against the above median group.

Public policy is not so direct in standard demographic-based systems, where promises are made to the below median income earners, but few reforms ever pass. In an income-based system of representation, every policy will have to have the benefits and interest spelled out in terms the below median income earners understand. When parties are less specialized, public policy is more ambiguous, with most of the benefits accumulating for the wealthy firm and landowners. In more specialized electorates, there isn't the comingling of interests or perspectives, forcing candidates to be more honest in the intent and more accurate with their promises.

Splitting the electorate by median income has another very important anti-corruption and class specific property. Candidates running for office in the below median income chamber must first qualify as having a below median income for the household. Those elected to office in the median chamber will have the same economic interests, incentives, and concerns of those which elected them, making it much more likely they only support policies that protect themselves and their constituents. One of the most deleterious effects of traditional demographic representation is the tendency for the political caste of elected and appointed official to accumulate vast fortunes while in office, serving the aristocratic classes and themselves, at the expense of the lower and middle classes. Most public policy favors the wealthy because our Senators and Representatives are also wealthy. Income-based representation makes this less likely by imposing eligibility criteria on the below median income chamber. When those candidates want to earn more money, they can leave the office and run for a seat in the above-median chamber.

The most important property of income-based representation split by a median coefficient is the adaptive anti-discriminatory attributes. If there is rampant institutional racism and substantial economic discrimination against minorities, women, or other vulnerable groups, it concentrates those voters and candidates within the below median income chamber where they are much more likely to acquire chairs of important oversight committees and majority control of the chamber. A minority, or group of minorities, only need a 26% share or the chamber, to impose majority control on their party members, and the institution. They may have to negotiate with their own party to maintain the majority power, but it will force the establishment or demographic majority party to win their support for every budget or appropriations passed from the above median income chamber.

Minority groups facing hiring and wage discrimination can leverage their majority control over one of the two chambers in a bicameral legislature to win civil rights and labor rights. Grass roots protests are only effective when it moves the legislature to reform, and that will be much easier when normal government operations can't continue unless those demands are met first. When wage and hiring discrimination ends for a minority group, the over-representation ends when their constituents are more evenly distributed between the two median income chambers. When the necessary laws are in place to protect minorities and women from exploitation or oppression, the legislature takes on conventional demographic representation, creating every incentive for the parties to end discrimination. No other contemporary representational system is as flexible and adaptable as median income-based representation, which makes it the best tool for nation building and reconstruction efforts.

Immediately after the Confederate states agree to an income-based system of representation, 5 or the 13 states in the original Confederacy (Mississippi, South Carolina, Georgia, Florida, and Texas) would transfer majority power to demographic-minority groups historically discriminated against within the state. Another 3 states (Virginia, North Carolina, and Alabama) are within just 1 or 2% points to providing vulnerable groups perpetual majorities in the below-median chamber[1].

Arizona and Nevada may have mixed political dispositions now, but with an income-based system of representation, minority groups would have 25% control over the below median income chamber. There is no way to estimate how a war will impact minority and majority group electorates, but other reconstruction reforms can focus on increasing voter turnout and registration, changing political preferences on the margins, which are typically younger and minority or poor voters, who are also the most likely victims during a crisis.

Texas and Florida already have majority minority control so nothing may change within those states, but Virginia, North Carolina, and Georgia are already trending Democratic, giving a reconstruction movement momentum. When the newly naturalized coming from immigrant enlistment, incentivized legal immigrants, or the enfranchisement of the undocumented, settles into these states, it could deliver the traditionally under-capitalized veteran and non-veteran populations to democratic parties. It must be stressed that only minority populations are calculated towards the below median majority, but a sizable portion of the white demographic-majority population caucuses with them, especially on labor and economic issues, which will bolster even modest cumulative proportions of minority populations. When combined, the more liberal and democratic constituents will likely have reliable and consistent control over the below median chamber, until labor laws and civil rights laws can dismantle the institution of systemic racism in the state, eliminating the need for over-representation in the below median chamber.

[1] See Table 37: Income-based Representation

It would be a major concession for the Confederate states to accept these terms, but they just might if they expect to preserve their institutional advantages within the federal government. Despite having their state legislatures split so they no longer have predictable trifectas, they will continue to maintain majorities in the federal Senate, Electoral College, and Constitutional Convention process. The Democratic party will see this as a concession on their part, knowing the demographic shift should change enough state-level elections to eventually break this monopoly up when the Caucasian population recede into minority-demographic group status. It is almost more important to change the culture and character of the states more than the structure of the federal institutions. When the states' constitutions are modified, it provides an opportunity to alter the electorate and all subsequent public policy and election outcomes for that region. Structural changes on the federal level merely mask or cover up the systemic cultural issues and don't prevent future authoritarian challenges from the states.

GDP-based or Income-based representation will be more appealing to former rebel states, if the largest and most urban cities have been emancipated. Not only does econometric representation lose its anti-discriminatory if the electorate is more homogenous, but the electorate that remains will be much more interested in class-based policies, after the cities gain independence and no longer participate in the state governments. There is much less pressure to adopt an income or GDP-based state legislature, if it doesn't break up the demographic groups' monopoly on state government, especially if the state is already rendered impotent by losing its wealthiest and most populous cities to the emancipation movement. The states could be forced to accept an econometric system of representation in order to preserve its access to the city's wealth and state tax revenues, but that would protect minority populations and eliminate any future threat.

Many of the Confederate states have cultures and histories predicated on systemic racism and with larger minority populations, the conversion to an income-based system of representation can be a powerful internal check on the state's ability to organize a subsequent secession or coup attempt. When political parties are at risk of organizing into authoritarian movements, it usually starts on the state level, where a demographic-majority imposes low-quality democratic entitlements which allows them to monopolize the governor and state legislature offices, giving them the ability to mobilize on the federal level. If Confederated states have econometric systems of representation imposed on them during reconstruction periods, they won't be able to engineer the certainty they need on the state level to predictably organize for a coup or secession.

An empowered demographic-minority group, with a majority in just one of the two bicameral legislatures could boycott all state level laws that would otherwise enable an authoritarian movement to prepare for war. Not only could the minority party prevent all war appropriations or borrowing during a conflict, but it could effectively prevent them organizing in the first place, by passing laws to change the culture years prior to a possible conflict. Rebellions must coordinate across many states and timed to maximize the chances of success, which makes the movement susceptible to disruptions. If just a few Confederate states can be constrained by changes in public finance laws or election laws, it will likely weaken the resolve of the movement by reducing the odds of success. As soon as an authoritarian movement is trying to manage resources across several election cycles, the odds change substantially when discriminated minority groups control a moderate number of the below median chambers.

An establishment party imposing an occupation government doesn't have to be overly concerned with equity, although it does promote better long-term outcomes when hostilities end and normalized trade and political discourse begins. One of the more aggressive strategies for imposing reconstruction on Confederate states repatriated after a conflict, is establishing a federal triangulation chamber on a representation coefficient based on net tax contributions. A states' federal tax contributions will be netted from the federal subsidies they receive, providing only those states with surplus contributions seats within the chamber. Although not fair by contemporary standards of high-quality modern democracy, it will be a useful implement to impose reconstruction on other states. It will never be accepted as a permanent institution considering the large number of allied states also excluded from admission to the chamber, but the federal budget ultimately determines fiscal policy, and which states receive more subsidies than the others, so the establishment party can dictate which states remain net surplus contributors. After the war, there will be substantial subsidies for reconstruction when cities must be rebuilt road by road and block by block. The institution can be imposed for a preset period, with the representational coefficients converted to another tax-based or equivalent term.

Using current federal tax subsidies and an estimate of revenues for the determining eligibility and magnitude of representation, it suggests 79% of the seats will be held by Democratic states and 21% held by Republican states, giving the Democrats the authority, they need to pass laws written by either of the other two chambers through reconciliation powers. The Democratic states projected to be in the majority for the chamber are Rhode Island, Delaware, Connecticut, Wisconsin, Washington, Minnesota, Massachusetts, Pennsylvania, New Jersey, Illinois, New York, and California[2]. The Republican states expected to have representation in the chamber are Wyoming, North Dakota, Indiana, Kansas, Arkansas, Nebraska, Ohio, and Texas. Only 20 of the current 50 states are represented, with 12 Democratic states and just 8 Republican states vying for majority control, making it a lower-quality form of representation, perfect for reconstruction periods, but not suitable for long term use, unless under a new colonial regime. The number of seats assigned to each state is based on the net federal tax revenues submitted, so even though Texas and Ohio are represented, the total number of Assemblymembers is limited.

A slightly more conventional and appropriate method for Net-tax representation is to leave the representational coefficient to be determined by population, while net taxes contributed is still used for eligibility. Even with demographic representation, the Republican states only gain 31% of the total seats within the chamber, making them a perpetual minority. Net-chambers are not empowered to write laws, but they can ratify laws coming from either of the other two chambers, giving the establishment party many more opportunities to exert majority control over the federal legislature. Under more extreme conditions, a Net-tax chamber can be given authority to operate as the federal triangulation chamber in regional government imposed during occupation and reconciliation. An establishment party will maintain majority control over the Net-tax chamber for as long as they want or need to, assuming they can easily pass appropriations and tax laws to preserve the

[2] See table 38: Net Federal Tax Chamber (Democratic)

power.

When the Net-tax chamber reverts to a traditional tax-based representation, delivering a number of seats equal to the gross amount of tax dollars contributed, without deducting the federal subsidies paid out. The wealthier states will still have a considerable advantage, but all states will have seats in the chamber making it more equitable and legitimate for long term use. When a tax-based representational coefficient is used, the Democrats have consistent and reliable 30% advantage in seats, acquiring nearly 57% of all representatives. Emancipated cities could raise this to 70%/30% advantage for Democrats, in average outcomes for an inter-state conflict.

Not all emancipated cities will be successful, not all will acquire statehood, and many won't ever challenge their state governments so the estimate will remain ambiguous, but each emancipated city will acquire its own representation while diminishing the seats allocated to the former state. Straight tax-based coefficients are identical to GDP-based representation in predictions of political dispositions, with many of the same expansionary properties.

Median tax-based coefficients have similar anti-discrimination properties as income-based representation, but one substantial concession is made to the formerly Confederate party. Tax-based Representation will be more acceptable to conservative parties because it is derivative of fiscal policy more than generalized economic performance, which means there is more direct control over how representation is apportioned across all state jurisdictions, and conservative parties show preferences and expertise in engineering more benefits for themselves. It will be interesting to see how the GOP responds to a political system dependent on fiscal policy, when they are usually averse to raising taxes on their core constituents. It should improve public policy and make the nation more viable, which is the only benefit of war.

The former Confederate party can't pursue their economic agendas without making sacrifices on which constituencies are forced to pay more taxes, to ensure the party is competitive in Assembly elections. It does give them a better chance for avoiding majority-minority below median chambers, but it will permanently change the substance and character of the party pursuing a fiscal agenda that no longer implicitly favors firms and wealthy families by reducing tax liabilities and maximizing profitability. Raising taxes will allow the nation to field larger more advanced militaries, provide more welfare for impoverished or exploited populations, and permit the state to enforce regulations on corporations.

Democratic allies in the occupied Confederate states acquire the possibility of stronger minority representation in the below tax liability chamber. However, tax-based representation is much more complicated in median partition because fiscal policy is much more malleable than an income-based system. Politicians can massage tax liabilities to favor certain demographics over others and produce fewer progressive institutions. Tax-based median partitions are a concession to an occupied state government, which initially provides power sharing between minorities and the demographic majority, but also permits future interventions the eliminate the discrimination, creating a purely demographic system of representation, or close enough where creative fiscal policy can produce useful advantages for an establishment party.

Each state's conservative political party are more proprietary with their agendas less exportable to other states. Provincial may be an even better descriptor. Every state will need a set on unique tax laws, conforming to a unique set of local employers and industries, that isn't easily transportable between states, even when neighboring. There will never be a single agenda that governs all the former Confederate states because each state will have to find a tax scheme that maximizes their own electoral chances for winning, while every state has different demographics, industrial compositions, and tax rates. A national agenda must appeal to the public, as well as the elected officials and wealthy families or firms donating campaign funds, which isn't easy when there is different special interest within each Confederate state.

1 MODELING INSTITUTIONS

Democracy is the most effective way to organize a nation politically. Public policy is designed and implemented according to the self-interests of the electorate. Through democracy, the people will be able to regulate themselves, tax themselves, and organize themselves. Democracy is the perpetual peaceful transfer of power between generations, parties, and persons. However, is contemporary democracy as efficient as it can be? The answer is no. Democracy can be reformed to improve the role identity of persons and political 31 quality invite challenges to the authority of the government. It will increase mistrust of the government, make it more susceptible to obstruction, and present perpetual crises for opportunists to exploit. Yet senates are found in most contemporary democracies. The reason is simple. Senates provide smaller states more representational power than larger states to entice the smaller states into political union. Smaller states feared their populations being subsumed by the larger states with little impact within a federal legislature or federal election. The senate assured these citizens they would not be marginalized in the new nation. It was the best solution to a complex problem considering the lack of expertise in statistics or political science.

There will always be a need for states to make concessions during nation building but now there are innovations in theory that will result in more equitable and balanced systems of representation. Statistical methods allow institutions to be created from measures of economy like GDP, tax liabilities, and income. These variables make excellent substitutes for senates and other forms of low quality democracy. The goal is to create a representational coefficient that complements or modifies the demographic-based representation without abjectly counteracting it such is the design of arbitrary systems of representation. Income-based representation is by far the most versatile and adaptable form of democratic government.

Income-based representation should not be confused with aristocracy or political corruption. Income-based representation does not infer the exploitation of the poor or the exaltation of the wealthy. The right to vote is not dependent on persons earning incomes. Universal Suffrage is distributed to the whole adult population. Nor do wealthier persons receive a larger number of votes than poorer persons. Each adult is apportioned exactly one vote. Those with no income or low income continue to vote with as much influence as a person with exorbitant wealth. Intuition is a dangerous tool if it isn't substantiated with evidence. Arguments against the higher quality econometric based systems of representation are simply without merit.

Political Institutions can be engineered by applying the measures of central tendency to economic concepts like income. Income is great target because it is neither exclusively personal or impersonal. Income applies to both individuals and groups of individuals simultaneously. The median income value can be used to separate a population evenly into two equal groups. One above median group and one below median group, each with an equal number of voters in the electorate. Income can also be used to separate districts and states into two similarly sized groups. Each district will be comprised of an equal number of voters and participate in the same number of elections. There is a third axis for representation for Income based representation. It can be used as a representational coefficient by states and nations forming political unions. This makes income-based representation a versatile component of any nation building exercise. It can be used in reform movements, nation building during occupations, and negotiations for political unions.

Statistics is a powerful tool for engineering high quality democratic entitlements in nations that might otherwise be overcome by partisan conflict along class, ethnic, or religious divides. The measures of central tendency can split groups into whole and symmetrical parts. This does more than simply create an impression of equality and fairness. All persons are included in the electorate preserving universal suffrage and self-governance. More importantly, applying the measures of central tendency to an electorate preserves proportional demographic representation. These are critical properties for legitimate and effective political systems. All voters must be treated equally and fairly for trust to be extended to the democratic government. The three organizational strategies for distributing income-based representation maintain these strict standards.

A micropolitical median partition uses personal income to divide the population into above median and below median parts. All states gain two sets of representatives, each set having a number of representatives equal to its proportional population. Despite separating individuals into two separate classes the chambers preserve proportional representation using a demographic based representational coefficient. This allows the median partition to capture the quality and legitimacy of a demographic system of representation and impart class-based themes into the political discourse. The class-based division promotes role specialization and better economic identity within each of the two median chambers.

A micropolitical median partition can use a national median income for partition or it can use a state median income for partition. A national median partition may split the states unevenly between the two chambers. One population will likely be larger than the other despite earning an equal number of representatives. This increases the representational ratio for one group creating an impression of representational inequality. However, the representational ratios in the median partition are far lower than representational ratios in conventional senates preserving its claim to legitimacy.

There is an implicit protection against wealth inequality producing more favorable ratios in the national median income partition. An imbalance in one state favoring the above median class will automatically be offset in another state with a representational ratio favoring the below median chamber. The nation continues to be split into two equal parts, allowing each state to be split unequally while the difference in conserved over the whole system. Deficiencies in representation for one class are compensated for surpluses in representation in another state. It is a balanced equation. The representational ratios of both chambers will equal exactly one when both are tallied and reconciled with each other.

A slight imbalance in representational ratios will produce a culture and impression of class identity within the state. The net representation between the classes will be equal, but each state may be more aligned with one class than the other. A state with twice as many below median voters (compared to national median) will continue to control only half the representatives but they will decide the majority of gubernatorial elections and other state-wide offices. This produces more opportunities for the electorate to identity and define themselves by the issues.

The nation has a second option for engineering its two adversarial chambers. The states could use their own state median income. This ensures that each state is always split precisely down the middle by a median value and each class-based chamber is supported by an equal number of voters. For this reason alone, the state median income partition is a more appropriate choice. There is no imbalance in representational ratios and thus no impression of favor. There is no weakness to be exploited by demagogues or by partisan political parties. It is more straight forward. It appears more honest and more accurate.

Voters are allocated to either the above median or below median income chambers. This is determined by evaluating the voters' average personal income from prior tax filings. The individuals' reported income is compared to the state or national median income. If their reported income is above the median value, they will vote in the above median income chamber. If their reported income is below the median value, they will vote in the above median income chamber. This includes persons with zero incomes providing the standard for universal suffrage.

Voter allocation may change from year to year depending on the income earned by the individual or family. The tax income history can be based on a single year. The state will have to prepare for a high revolution rate for voters switching from one chamber to another year after year. This can be expensive and introduce a large number of bureaucratic errors into the voter registration system. Instead, states can employ strategies to smooth out the variation or rate of change from year to year. One method is to use an average of 3 or 5 years to determine the voter eligibility. This should cut down on the annual fluctuation in wages and any revolving eligibility. Another option is set the timeframe equal to the length of the term for the elected office.

Every year, the tax agency will produce the median value used to separate the two classes and register them. Every year, the taxpayer's average income is calculated and compared to the new aggregate average income. This ensures that wage inflation does not corrupt the result and skew participation in the two median chambers. Citizens are then allocated to one of the two chambers based on the prior years' tax results. If they don't file timely, a temporary value will be substituted based on the prior average. However, all elected officials are required to file by a due date set by the state they originate from.

The macropolitical median partition continues to divide the population by class, but this classification occurs on the state or district level. This partition separates the states or districts into above median and below median chambers depending on their median income. In many respects, this is a sounder organizational strategy as it produces more diverse electorates without an emphasis on personal economic identity. Elections are less predictable in electorates that include voters in all income brackets. This also substitutes state-class identity for familial-class identity which should avoid more sectarian conflict.

The median income value is determined during the 10-year Census and it remains static until the next Census. The states are ordered sequentially from highest median income to lowest median income and the population is split equally in two. Half of the states or districts are admitted into the above median chamber and the other half are admitted into the below median chamber. Each state continues to receive a number of representatives equal to their population (although substitutes for demographic representational coefficients could be used). There may be one state split in two un equal parts but otherwise each state participates in only one chamber.

Macropolitical median partitions aggregate voters into larger regions. This imbues more diversity into each electorate. A district with a below median income will contain a large cross section of individuals and family with incomes that range from abject poverty to aristocratic wealth. There will be a larger number of poorer persons but persons with above median incomes will still be present. All persons vote in the same district for the same representative. This should average out electoral outcomes and produce more moderate candidates. Representatives must try to appeal to both classes simultaneously ruling out more extreme rhetoric and policy agendas. In Micropolitical median partitions, the candidates are dedicated to electorates exclusively comprised of either above median or below median voters. This makes them far more homogenous in their electoral output.

Constituencies will adapt by becoming more comfortable with rhetoric that may not personally benefit them or that challenges their personal belief systems. This will promote the exchange of ideas between constituents of different classes promoting a healthier and more mature electorate. However, voter tendencies will continue to be present, and a below median income district will favor candidates that speak more directly about issues concerning the poor and rural communities. Above median income districts will favor candidates who speak to their urban core values and belief systems. Districts may aggregate diversity but the average output matters. Macropolitical representation is a consensus-based system and therefore dependent on majority rule.

The residents of a single district or state all vote in the same election for the same candidates. This introduces themes of an urban and rural divide into the political landscape. The above median chamber will include more urban areas with higher median incomes while the below median chamber will include rural areas with lower median incomes. Urban areas tend to be more ethnically diverse and more secular. They tend to be better educated and wealthier. Rural jurisdictions tend to be more homogenous, with less education, less earnings, and have a greater dependence on religious institutions. Although this looks divisive, the geo-spatial properties of macropolitical income-based representation will disrupt traditional regional affiliations by splitting the jurisdictions between the two chambers.

It should be noted that the median income is not a measurement of GDP, so the total quantity of GDP will not be split evenly between the two chambers. No implicit economic advantage exists for the individual districts with the highest median incomes resulting in a more appropriate and fair distribution of political power and economic power. Median income may be completely independent of accumulated GDP, randomizing the amount of wealth found in each of the two median chambers This should engender more support for a Macropolitical median income partition when nation building.

The third organizational method uses a representational coefficient based on median income and population to determine the number of representatives apportioned to each state. The formula is ((median income x population) / (sum of all median income x population results divided by number of seats)). Representatives are allocated to each state based on the representational coefficient with all elected to the same institution. The system continues to be correlated to population imbuing it with the legitimacy other demographic systems maintain but it also emphasizes wealth equality. States with higher median incomes will have proportionally more representation in the legislature. States with less wealth inequality will be able to export their economic policies to states with higher wealth inequality, promoting political stability and with luck raw economic activity. GDP based systems of representation don't guarantee that states with lower wealth inequality have more representation and therefore shouldn't be as successful as those based on median incomes.

This configuration of income-based representation is more familiar than a median partition and will be easier to justify during an occupation or reformation. It only requires one chamber leaving a second to be used for demographic representation or senatorial representation. Therefore, it is the most likely to be implement after conflicts during nation building or reform movements. This preserves the historic structure of the democracy while updating its representational methodology. If the structure of democracy contributes to more wealth equality, it will increase the odds the nation perseveres through the inevitable periods of instability fledgling nations experience.

This arrangement is a concession to states with more wealth equality. States with higher median wages will have incrementally more representation than states with low median wages. More populous states will continue to have more proportional representation than smaller states, but it will be modified by the median income. However, this arrangement also allows less populous states with higher median wages to earn disproportionate representation in the chamber. More importantly, the median value can be improved over time with policy finesse and expertise. It is the perfect concession when negotiating newly incorporated nations or political unions. The representational coefficient emphasizes both economic prowess and fairness and can be improved with effort, randomizing future performance in more competitive political markets.

The democratization movement will benefit from another option in its repertoire. An income-based system of representation is a concession to both small states and large states with higher median incomes. It cuts across regional and sectarian divides by offering another axis for agreement. Its reliance on median incomes allows it to scale up with a nation as it moves from developing nation to mature economy. Poorer and more rural states may accept the terms on the expectation of increasing median incomes and thus net representation in the system. Median income can be manufactured with public policy changing the allocation of representatives within the union. States may value this property more than any static benefit provided by a conventional senate or demographic based representational coefficient.

2 RHETORIC FOR CHANGE

Income-based representation using a micropolitical method for organization preserves the authority and legitimacy of demographic-based representational coefficients while maintaining a bicameral legislative process. The most effective income-based systems will employ a mechanism called a median partition. A median partition splits the electorate into an above median chamber and a below median chamber. Citizens are ranked in order of income through tax forms and then split by the median value. The median partition honors the tenants of universal suffrage and majority rule by accepting demographic representational coefficients.

The two class-based chambers are coequal with an equivalent number of elected officials and similar oversight and legislative powers. This imparts legitimacy by ensuring that the constituents of one chamber have as much influence as another. This is critical for all institutions in a democracy but especially for one build upon class distinctions. Using demographic representation coefficients ensures the nation continues to be governed by consensus, allowing the electorate to successful regulate itself with a high degree of accuracy and honesty

Senates protected minority states' rights but the median partition will protect individual minority rights. In discriminatory environments, the median partition offers minority populations a significant boost to representational power without diminishing the accuracy of the overall representational system. By splitting the population into two coequal parts of a bicameral legislative process, minorities and other vulnerable populations can effectively double their representational power in a single chamber. If a demographic group is discriminated against in terms of employment and wages, they will be concentrated within the below median income chamber greatly improving their electoral power. Demographic groups facing discrimination will be able to coerce more concessions from the majority party by obstructing laws or offering other legislation for trade.

However, once the discrimination ends, the minorities will lose their representational advantages. In this respect it makes Income-based representation reactive. This property incentivizes majority demographic groups to pass policies that distribute wages and income more fairly, thus ensuring they retain the majority of political power. With less discrimination present in the economy, minority demographic groups will be more satisfied with the natural constraints democracy and majority rule imposes on them.

There is another major advantage to income-based representation. The median income partition will ensure that as economic conditions deteriorate due to wealth inequality or other deficiencies, the experiences and attitudes of the representatives will shift in favor of reform. For example, if wages are stagnant for a decade and costs continue to rise, a larger number of middle class wage earners in the above median chamber will identify with public policy that is supported by the below median chamber. This will increase cooperation and coordination between the two chambers.

Demographic systems of representation tend to obfuscate the interests of their representatives and conflate issues beyond recognition. Their constituents often rely on tribalism to differentiate themselves and this contribute to hyper-partisan environments during war or economic crisis. The poor will identify with the owners' class on issues of ethnicity or religions and support them despite the lack of economic sympathies. Political party affiliation is transmitted through parents, through community, and through profession. It is predictable that society will homogenize around ethnicity rather than economy.

This diminishes the probability of successfully reforming the economy. Without support for economic reforms intended to reverse wealth inequality and improve labor rights, the public will be susceptible to populism or fascism. Conditions will exacerbate, and the nation risks a challenge to its sovereignty. The nation will enter a period of decline when it stops making investments into infrastructure, education, and social insurance. Sectarian differences will become pronounced and radicals will start threatening debt defaults and government shutdowns. Unless the opposition party can pass economic reforms correcting the wealth inequality and worsening economic corrections, the democratic nation may suffer a rebellion, secession, or usurpation

Class-based representation cuts through this artificial barrier. It splits the industrial aristocracy found in in the 4th income quartile from the working poor in the 1st income quartile. It will be the intervening variable in our continued experiment in democracy. If the richest 25% can't depend on implicit electoral support from the poorest 25%, then they may not be able to resist the economic reforms that would dispel the populist insurgence. The middle 50% of the electorate will dominate electoral output in the legislatures when the 1st and 4th income quartiles are partitioned from each other. The middle class will dictate which policies are pursue by the political parties. Class-based representation should prove more durable than demographic representation over longer terms due to its ability to identify and address economic issues more easily.

At first impression, income-based representation looks as though it would provoke the fervor of populism, but this conclusion is inaccurate. The bicameral process is more likely to completely obstruct any populist policies coming out of an institution. If the below median chamber is pursuing public policy that redistributes wealth in a rash or haphazard manner, the owners class and investors class can block the legislation with the concentrated power in the above median chamber. The same is true for anti-democratic coming from the industrial aristocracy that policies that might interfere with honest and accurate elections. Either chamber could effectively block the legislative output protecting again any extreme movement to the right or the left.

There is another powerful constraint on populism. The concentration of minorities in one of the chambers will present the most effective obstacle to a party seeking to marginalize citizens or usurp the democratic process. Minorities will already be organized with a bully pulpit to resist an overly aggressive majority demographic group. They will have a legitimate platform dedicated to protecting their civil liberties and political interests. Oppressed minority groups will have a disproportionate amount of political representation in the below median income chamber, granting them leadership positions, committee chair positions, investigative powers, and access to the deliberative process and due process. These innate protections might be critical in diffusing the anger, anxiety, or enthusiasm inherent in a populist movement. Even a delay in implementation may cool the animal spirits inherent in populism.

Populism is a predatory movement. The probability of resurgence is derivative of the probability of success. If a majority demographic group can pass discriminatory laws and participate in pogroms with little resistance, the frequency and severity of events will increase. Once a minority group can defend themselves with political capital or military might, the incentives towards conflict will diminish. The higher the material or emotional costs of conflict, the less rewarding it is and the most likely the majority demographic group will negotiate on power sharing and improving due process. If the minority groups recognize the threat early enough and organize to resist it, they will increase the odds of avoiding the conflict. If minority groups don't identify the threat and move to counter it, they could quickly find themselves in an inferior position with less civil liberties and no access to the institutional means to defend the community.

There may be an extended period of time when the majority demographic group can predict the loss of political power and try and resist the peaceful transfer of power. The majority population can consolidate political power and censor political dialogue from all legislative chambers. A majority in a demographic chamber could impose restricted electorates, suppress minority voters, disenfranchise others through mass incarceration and pass a whole host of anti-democratic policies. They can redistribute wealth from the employee classes and consumer classes to the owners class and the investors class. This will stoke anger in a frustrated middle and lower classes increasing the xenophobia and fear of minorities. Majority demographic groups can easily defund the government with regressive taxes, austerity measures, and tax breaks for the wealthy. This weakened government will be susceptible to threats of default on the government's debts or permanently shut down the government.

Demographic-based legislatures are especially susceptible to populism. Demographic-based representation can crowd out the economic interests of minority groups or other special interest groups more easily than if the populations were split by incomes and class. Income-based representation is an exceptional check on populism by isolating the interests and providing institutional recourse for the opposition. This is true whether the populist impulse comes from the below median or above median chambers. Most median partitions provide demographic representation in addition to the class-based representation. It is an improvement on traditional democracy, not a substitute. Proportional representation is the highest quality of democratic entitlements. It confers legitimacy to the political system, which is a critical element when diffusing populism and mitigating uprisings from distressed minority populations.

Income-based representation can prove itself to be superior to demographic-based representation by isolating the economic interests of both groups and dedicating labor for their advocacy. It is presumed that the class identity will allow more citizens to more effectively evaluate their own interests and vote in pursuit of them. One of the more important attributes of classed representation is the eligibility criteria for representatives. The elected representatives in the below median chamber will be required to maintain wages less than the median wage. This ensures that their advocacy is accurate and honest. The representatives will have the same economic pressures as their constituents. They will have more similar upbringings and social networks. They will be from the same universities and same neighborhoods. Income-based representation promotes a high quality agency between elected officials and their constituencies unlike those representatives in conventional demographic systems.

In legislatures like those found in the United States, Senators and Representatives are paid close to 3x the median wage[3]. The median net wealth for a legislator is 14x that of an ordinary citizen[4]. It is incredulous that this official has the same economic interests as their constituents. They aren't worried about minimum wage laws, they don't use public transportation, they don't shop at second hand stores, and they don't have to make critical decisions about rent or food on a daily basis.

The agency relationship is lost in translation. The representatives care for these programs in theory but are more willing to suffer program cuts and patiently wait out extended periods without reform or improvement. A political party could wait 12-16 years before raising the minimum wage which might represent nearly 40% of the below median wage earners income. This is barley advocacy. It certainly isn't agency. The below median class needs representation that suffers the same economic

---

[3] "Median Income," U.S. Census, accessed March 10th, 2018.
https://www.census.gov/searchresults.html?q=median+income&page=1&stateGeo=no
ne&searchtype=web&cssp=SERP&search.x=0&search.y=0
[4] Danielle Kurtzleben, "Let them eat cake," U.S. News. Last modified Jan 9th, 2014.
https://www.usnews.com/news/blogs/data-mine/2014/01/09/let-them-eat-cake-
members-of-congress-14-times-more-wealthy-than-average-american

pressures or discrimination they do. This is the only way to achieve accurate and honest representation.

Wages are rarely equitably distributed with the economy. There are tremendous differences between incomes earned and wealth accumulated between demographic groups and genders. Discrimination produces higher rates of unemployment and lower wages for vulnerable populations. Wealth is often transmitted through generations by nepotism or cronyism. People tend to hire people that look like the, talk like them, and act like them. They promote these people faster and they give them more bonuses and higher raises.

Often, there are barriers of entry to certain professions. for minorities and women. This results in systemic wealth inequality too. Look at the disparate value social workers and teacher provide compared to their below average incomes. Look at the value psychologists and counselors provide compared to their median wage performance. Many critical roles for professionals are undervalued in the economy but produce some of the best candidates for political office.

Economy tends to underpay minorities and women resulting in barriers to election in legislatures that don't separate the above median wage earners from the below median wage earners. This will all change when voter eligibility is based on income eligibility. Those professionals already accustomed to median wages won't feel encumbered by the wage restrictions. They won't feel disparaged by the median wage provided during office. They will continue to experience the same economic pressures their constituents suffer and will be better suited to satisfy the representational demands of office.

The below median chamber will have the same oversight and appropriations powers as the above median chamber. This will contribute to exceptional government sector experience which may lead to other roles in the public sector. For those representatives who choose to stay, it will have all the prestige of a coequal branch in government. For those who choose to leave, it could lead to speaking engagements, book deals, appointments to corporate boards, or highly paid private sector jobs.

Representatives who want to earn more than the median wage can leave office and pursue their dreams. Public service is voluntary, and they can leave office after their term or resign. If they value money more than power, there are no long-term consequences other than ineligibility for office in the below median chamber. They can even choose to seek office in the above median chamber at some future point. They will have to start over. They risk losing their office and then failing to secure a higher income. It is ultimately their decision. The above median income electorate includes many middle-class wage earners. Their new constituents may value the history of success as the representatives climbs the economic classed social ladder.

There are enough economic incentives for persons to become below median income representatives to justify maintaining the income eligibility for the office. The median income provided by the office is either replacement for other median income or improvement in 1st quartile income. Those who already earn more than the median income will seek office in the above median income chamber. This is a difference in difference calculation. Below median income earners will be more than satisfied with maintaining a below median income when they had no expectations to earn more.

A teacher or social worker earning $43,000 a year will see the benefit in earning $72,000 as a below median representative. A psychologist or therapist earning $66,000 will earn nearly the same amount but gain prestige and power from being a representative. It is more important work that imparts valuable skills to the office holder. It is fully expected that most representative will continue to serve despite the income restriction. There is an unmistakable tradeoff. They can either pursue wealth or thy can serve their nation in the below median income chamber. They can't do both. The more avaricious or ambitious representative can always choose to pursue an above median income office later but must relinquish their current elected office first.

Income eligibility for representatives will promote the below median electorate to work for itself rather than depend on charity from the owners classes. The representatives will live in the same communities and make comparable amounts of money. These shared economic sympathies will make the representatives work harder for more economic concessions that benefit the 1st and 2nd income quartiles. It is a form of ownership. The property is class identity. It is like any other small business or form of self-employment. When the below median representatives pass pro-union, laws raising middle class wages, they will share in the profit. When the below median representative pursues more progressive taxes, they will personally benefit from lower effective tax rate on middle incomes. When the below median representative set a higher minimum wage, the larger volume of circulating dollars will benefit their communities.

The below median chamber will run like a modern corporation, seeking to maximize returns for 1st and 2nd income quartile wage earners. It will be a firm run by the community for the community's benefit. These are the exact same motivations the wealthy have for participating in democratic government. They relentlessly pursue tax laws that benefit them exclusively. They seek to restrain pollution laws that would restrict their market share and increase operating costs. They strive for the loosest of labor laws to ensure the lowest cost commodities. The wealthy have always used the government as a tool to protect their monopolies, their rents, their property. The below median classes will benefit from the higher order organization a median partition provides. They will enjoy the same financial incentives the wealthiest citizens in democracy have enjoyed for hundreds of years. Income based representation will split the world in twain and elevate the median class and workers class to an equal position as the wealthy and aristocratic classes.

Below median reps will have their transportation and quarters paid for by the state with the state regulating the standards or requirements. This will help bridge the gap in compensation between the above median and below median chambers while preserving the quality of the agency below median reps have with below median electorate. The representative shouldn't be penalized for working at the capitol when they earn a similar income as most other wage earners in their district and those wage earners don't have those transportation costs. The representative should have an equivalent lifestyle to those in the district.

The representative should have similar disposable incomes, savings rates, retirement programs and health benefits. This will align the below median income representative with the economic interests of their constituents. If they face the same education costs and real estate costs when constrained by the same income, they will pursue policy that relieves those stressors. Most constituents don't have to spend weeks or months lodging in a foreign city, so those costs should be borne by the state they represent or a national subsidy. The institution paying for the transportation and lodgings can set standards for the services. If necessary, the institution or state can acquire the infrastructure or assets needed to provide the transportation and lodgings.

There is no evidence to suggest that persons from higher income brackets provide better leadership, especially when the vehicle for that responsibility pays a wage 3x that of its median constituent[5]. For most of recorded history, the legislators were part of the aristocracy. They were the landlords and employers of the public. They enjoyed considerable economic power which translated into political power during the transition to democracy. The United States certainly had wealth requirements for voting at its. All of the ancient democracies had restricted electorates based on land ownership. Our insistence on paying our legislators 3x the median wage or 12x the minimum wage is a vestige of prior periods with lower quality democracy or monarchy[6]. This must inception end.

Establishing a wage requirement for the below median chamber doesn't encumber the above median chamber. Wealthier people can continue to seek office and represent themselves and their class. They can pay their representatives a wage far higher than the below

---

[5] "Median Income," U.S. Census, accessed March 10th, 2018.
https://www.census.gov/search-results.html?q=median+income&page=1&state-Geo=none&searchtype=web&cssp=SERP&search.x=0&search.y=0

[6] "Median Income," U.S. Census, accessed March 10th, 2018.
https://www.census.gov/searchresults.html?q=median+income&page=1&state-Geo=none&searchtype=web&cssp=SERP&search.x=0&search.y=0

median income chamber's wage. However, when they start talking about tax breaks for other wealthy people and for deregulating labor laws, it will be more transparent. The below median class will be able to identify the economic initiative as coming from owners' class or investors class. They will immediately be able to disambiguate the source of the policy. Hopefully, this will help them recognize their own interests. The below median chamber will have an opportunity to vote on every bill. They will scrutinize every law that is passed by the above median chamber and see it through the prism of class. It should revitalize the consumer movements and labor movements and bring accountability back to the public sector.

The United States' legal system has a long history of an adversarial structure with plaintiffs squaring off with defendants in a process that involves agency protections from counsel. The United States' political system never adopted the same rigid adversarial structure as court systems despite promoting the behavior with a party system. Political Party agendas are less cohesive than a distinct economic class. The members of a political party will make concessions to another political party more quickly and more often when they stand to personally benefit from the agreement. The leadership of political parties are simply more likely to have higher incomes and more accumulated wealth. This conflict in motivation or consequence contributes to the natural gradient towards elitist public policy. This defect in agency creates mistrust of the government and it invites dangerous corrections in the political market.

The political parties are adversarial, but this is a far weaker relationship than setting two institutions in opposition. It is evident through the pace of reform and quality of reform that the current party system is deficient. The nation would be better off with a more formal system of adversarial politics relying on institutions. This can be accomplished with class-based representation. The below median income chamber will have its own leadership, and all elected officials will have median incomes. There will be no coercion by wealthier party members. There will be no personal incentives for taking money from corporations or special interest groups with contrary policy agendas.

The agent-principal relationship will preserve its integrity through the income constraints and bicameral legislative process. This relationship has always existed for the above median classes. Most elected officials earned 13x as much as the poorest and 3 or 4x as much as the median wage earner. This implicitly aligned them with the owner's class and the investors class. The representatives shared more economic sympathies with the wealthy and thus were their agents. Any economic reform passed were due to tradition or charity, rather than an integral agent-principal relationship. There primary loyalties were too themselves and their households, not to the electorate. Nobody can serve two masters equally well. There are always conflicts in principles and principals.

The median partition is more adversarial than any party system. The incentives for the below median chamber will be set into opposition to the interests of the above median income chamber. They will check each other's rasher sentiments. No laws will pass without the expressed consent of the other class. There will be no opportunity for the animal spirits of populism to gain traction in both chambers. Nor will the owners class and investors class be able to extract undue rents by passing exploitative laws and property rights.

The biggest threat to equitable economy will be obstruction. An owners class and investors class could refuse to negotiate on labor laws and tax laws, but this will strain the economy and make its markets unstable. Without the implicit support of the below median class, there will be no bailouts during an economic emergency or market correction. It would be mutually ensured suicide if the above median chamber did not negotiate in good faith with the below median chamber for economic reforms and due process. Don't forget, most financial incentives will remain on the balance sheet of the above median chamber. They will benefit more from an equitable economy and be willing to make concessions to keep the profits flowing.

In democracy, the median voter has most of the political power but in income-based representation there is a median voter within each chamber. This shifts more political power to the poorer citizens who would normally be less represented in a single electorate. In the United States 12.7% of all adults are considered to be in poverty. In a conventional demographic chamber, this group would get little more than lip service. The agency is at a distance. There is concern but no real familiarity or identity with the poor. This changes in a median partition. This 12.7% will occupy nearly 25.4% of the below median income chamber. Suddenly, this demographic group can sway local elections and influence legislative output. The median voter with the chamber will be the upper half of the 1st income quartile and the lower half of the 2nd income quartile. This is far different than the median voter found in demographic chambers.

The below median income chamber will contain zero entries which will drag down the median value. In the United States, this is only about 7.9% of all persons and the group is primarily made up of persons on disability, students, and unemployed[7]. They act as placeholders and occupy a small portion of the below median values in the below median chamber. The median partition concentrates political power and this segment will acquire roughly 15.8% of all representational power in the chamber. They will be a strong coalition partner intent on protecting entitlement spending and fiscal policy that benefits the students, the unemployed, and the disabled. Almost everybody else in the United States works or is in a household with a working partner.

There are far more income earners in the above median chamber resulting in output that is farther away from the median voter than the output of the below median chamber. There are at least 7.9% more wage earners and their wages are considerably higher than the average wage earned in below median chamber. The above median chamber also has far more outliers that impact the average of the above median income chamber. This produces a regressive shift towards the poorer part of the two median quartiles (median class).

For instance, an electorate with a median income of $54k might be split in two with one median reduced to $39k and the other median raised to $82k. The difference in attitudes or preferences between the 54k median and the $39k median will be much less severe than the change in preferences from the $54k median and the $82k median. Each part of the bicameral median partition has

---

[7] Brad Plumer, "Who doesn't pay taxes, in eight charts," *The Washington Post*, last modified Sept 18, 2012.
https://www.washingtonpost.com/news/wonk/wp/2012/09/18/who-doesnt-pay-taxes-in-charts/?noredirect=on&utm_term=.d3989fade602

its own output derivative of the median voter. Laws from the two chambers must then be reconciled. This will allow poorer persons to exert more influence over the entire electorate than if they continued to participate within a single electorate of $72k median income.

When economic conditions deteriorate, average cost inflation outpaces wage inflation and a larger portion of the above median electorate will share economic sympathies and stressors with the below median electorate. Disposable incomes for those with $82k can absorb wage loss and inflation in food, shelter, and healthcare far better than those with $39k or $54k. The disposable income of those with 54k might be half that of those earning $82k. Even a few years of wage stagnation might produce drastic changes in disposable incomes for the $39k or $54k wage earners. Economy is the motivating force behind most reform and role specialization in the electorate should help facilitate the reform process. The electorate will continue to be divided into two equal parts but a larger number in both chambers will experience the wage loss or inflation and support economic reforms intended to correct the imbalance.

The below median income chamber is far more susceptible to economic disruptions and will therefore be the source of more attempts to reform it. The above median chamber will respond to this leadership when the risk of non-action outweighs the loss in regulation and reform. The 4th income quartile could resist the reform movement in the above median chamber, but this will cause the economic conditions to deteriorate even more. The longer it takes to reform the economy and the worse the conditions, the more radical the electorate gets. The 4th income quartile stands to lose more market share, more equity, and more property if the middle class is moved towards more reactionary policies.

A traditional demographics-based electorate relies on the majority experience. A majority is far more likely to adjust favorably to wage loss or other negative economic trends by virtue of larger disposable incomes prior to the shift. A loss of 10% in wages over a 10-year period for the 1st income quartile might be equated with a loss of 90% of their disposable incomes and savings while the same 10% loss in wages for the 2nd or 3rd income quartile might only cause a 20% loss in disposable income or savings. The middle class can ignore the issue until conditions become so untenable that the bottom 80% of the income distribution is threatened. Obviously, this only happens during severe contractions. The 1st and 2nd income quartiles are likely to suffer under a conventional demographic system.

However, a median partition concentrates the political power of the 1st income quartile. They represent nearly 50% of the below median chamber and if the median class starts to lose disposable incomes due to wage stagnation or excessive inflation, they the median voter will more closely align and form a majority with the lower income voters. The 1st income quartile represents nearly 50% of the below median chamber and losing 10% of their gross to inflation would motivate them to pass higher minimum wages, pro-union laws, and other reforms that will raise their incomes. If only a small margin of those in the 2nd income quartile supports them, they will have majority political power in the below median income chamber. They can then force concessions from the above median chamber by obstructing government. If the political market is competitive, an opposition party will win majority in the above median chamber at least half the time, providing a pathway to reform for the below median chamber.

This will make the political system more responsive to the needs of the 1st income quartile. When the poorer citizens have more political power, they can address issues after they are identified far more quickly than waiting for the complete collapse of economic conditions to provoke a reaction from the above median income population. This checks the implicit slant towards elitism found in most contemporary democracies. It emphasizes the role of the employee class and consumer class in a political system that would otherwise over represent the owners class and investors class. This method for representation acts to balance out the other economic and political forces that have resulted in the under representation and exploitation of the under classes.

This is especially true when discrimination plays a part in oppressing minority and gender groups by lack of access to living wages and other benefits like healthcare and retirement. Although societies may make declarations about equality it is in the revealed preferences of wage and wealth distributions that depict the actual quality of emancipation and suffrage. These figures and facts will contradict the stated preferences of those determining wages and fiscal policy within the economy. Revealed preferences are always much more accurate than stated preferences and income-based representation will help correct the inaccuracies in reporting found in most contemporary democracies.

3 THE POLITICS OF DISCRIMINATION

The assignment of wages is often arbitrary or rife with discrimination. Most wages are determined by a very small group of employers whose judgement is often conflicted with biases or a motivation to suppress labor costs. This discretion is susceptible to discrimination based on race, ethnicity, religion, gender, or criminal history. It is also susceptible to the profit motive. An employer will hire employees at the minimum wage, regardless of the how low the wage is relatively to other wages in the economy, and without consideration if wage is falling relative to inflation. Most employers minimize their labor costs to attitude maximize their own profits indicating a coercive or exploitative.

Providing a structural representational advantage to the below median income earners will counter this unavoidable but otherwise inaccurate valuation of those persons. Many of the conditions resulting in their low compensation are situational rather than causal, and the political market should correct this natural inequity with a regressive tendency in representation. Don't forget, the above median chamber has as much political power as the below median chamber, but the population would have otherwise been subsumed by the majority demographic group. The bicameral process in the median partition creates this added value for minority groups, regardless of which gender, ethnicity or religion those vulnerable groups are. As soon as a minority group acquires majority status, they lose that innate advantage.

If women and minorities are concentrated in the below median chamber it indicates a strong prevalence of discriminatory policies in the economy. If the above median chamber routinely resists passing policies that would help ameliorate this condition, then the public and the media can more clearly describe it as gender discrimination or racial discrimination. The identification of these trends should shame more above median voters into supporting candidates that advocate for more egalitarian policies. Shame is a powerful motivator. Even an impression of discrimination could convince more elected representatives to support the measures. This is especially true in nations with longer histories of voter suppression, wage exploitation, or other abuses. When the wage or employment discrimination ends, women and minorities will be dispersed equally among the chambers and no separate gender or race identity will exist.

Income-based representation protects minority rights far better than demographic systems of representation. By splitting the electorate in two equal parts, where each chamber has equal representation, it effectively doubles the political power of minorities. A minority group with an incidence rate of 16% within the nation, might have 32% of the total representation in the below median chamber if that group is routinely discriminated against regarding wages and employment. If the minority group is not discriminated against, it will have maximum dispersion between the two chambers (half the population in the above median chamber and half the population in the below median chamber). Whenever there aren't normally distributed incomes in the minority population, it will concentrate political power in the below median chamber.

For example, in the United States the average wage for all households is $53,657 but the average wage for African Americans is just $35,398[8] [9]. Approximately 63.7% of African Americans fall under $50,000 which greatly improves their representation in the below median chamber[10]. The total proportion of African Americans in the U.S. population is 13.2% but they will acquire almost 16.8% of the below median chamber for a 27.4% increase in representation[11]. Hispanics populations have a median wage of $42,491 and occupy 15.3% of the overall population[12] [13]. Nearly 56.6% of Hispanics fall under $50,000 allowing them to acquire nearly 17.3% of the

---

[8] DeNavas-Walt, Carmen, and Proctor, Bernadette (September, 2015). Income and Poverty in the United States: 2014. P.14. U.S. Census Bureau.
Retrieved from https://www.census.gov/content/dam/Census/library/publications/-2015/demo/p60-252.pdf

[9] DeNavas-Walt, Carmen, and Proctor, Bernadette (September, 2015). Income and Poverty in the United States: 2014. P.14. U.S. Census Bureau.
Retrieved from https://www.census.gov/content/dam/Census/library/publications/-2015/demo/p60-252.pdf

[10] DeNavas-Walt, Carmen, and Proctor, Bernadette (September, 2015). Income and Poverty in the United States: 2014. P.14. U.S. Census Bureau.
Retrieved from https://www.census.gov/content/dam/Census/library/publications/-2015/demo/p60-252.pdf

[11] Sandra Colby, and Jennifer Ortman. (March 2015). Projections of the size and Composition of the U.S. Populations: 2014 to 2060. P.9. U.S. Census Bureau. Retrieved from
https://www.census.gov/content/dam/Census/library/publications/2015/demo/p25-1143.pdf

[12] Carmen DeNavas-Walt, and Bernadette Proctor. (September, 2015). Income and Poverty in the United States: 2014. P.14. U.S. Census Bureau. Retrieved from https://www.census.gov/content/dam/Census/library/publications/-2015/demo/p60-252.pdf

[13] Sandra Colby, and Jennifer Ortman. (March 2015). Projections of the size and Composition of the U.S. Populations: 2014 to 2060. P.9. U.S. Census Bureau. Retrieved from
https://www.census.gov/content/dam/Census/library/publications/2015/demo/p25-1143.pdf

below median chamber for a 13.2% increase in representation[14] [15]. Native Americans add roughly 1.5% to the proportion of minorities in the below median chamber when it is estimated their median wage is equivalent to African Americans and they account for 1.2% of overall population[16] [17]. Asians add another 3.7% after accounting for 5.4% of the population earning a median wage of $74,297 with only 34.3% falling below the $50,000 threshold[18] [19] [20].

Together, African Americans, Hispanics, Asians, and Native Americans are 35.1% of the total population but acquire 39.4% of the seats[21]. This is 77.2% of the seats

---

[14] Carmen DeNavas-Walt, and Bernadette Proctor. (September, 2015). Income and Poverty in the United States: 2014. P.14. U.S. Census Bureau. Retrieved from https://www.census.gov/content/dam/Census/library/publications/-2015/demo/p60-252.pdf

[15] Carmen DeNavas-Walt, and Bernadette Proctor. (September, 2015). Income and Poverty in the United States: 2014. P.17. U.S. Census Bureau. Retrieved from https://www.census.gov/content/dam/Census/library/publications/-2015/demo/p60-252.pdf

[16] Carmen DeNavas-Walt, and Bernadette Proctor. (September, 2015). Income and Poverty in the United States: 2014. P.34. U.S. Census Bureau. Retrieved from https://www.census.gov/content/dam/Census/library/publications/-2015/demo/p60-252.pdf

[17] Sandra Colby, and Jennifer Ortman. (March 2015). Projections of the size and Composition of the U.S. Populations: 2014 to 2060. P.9. U.S. Census Bureau. Retrieved from https://www.census.gov/content/dam/Census/library/publications/2015/demo/p25-1143.pdf

[18] Sandra Colby, and Jennifer Ortman. (March 2015). Projections of the size and Composition of the U.S. Populations: 2014 to 2060. P.9. U.S. Census Bureau. Retrieved from https://www.census.gov/content/dam/Census/library/publications/2015/demo/p25-1143.pdf

[19] Carmen DeNavas-Walt, and Bernadette Proctor. (September, 2015). Income and Poverty in the United States: 2014. P.36. U.S. Census Bureau. Retrieved from https://www.census.gov/content/dam/Census/library/publications/-2015/demo/p60-252.pdf

[20] Carmen DeNavas-Walt, and Bernadette Proctor. (September, 2015). Income and Poverty in the United States: 2014. P.14. U.S. Census Bureau. Retrieved from https://www.census.gov/content/dam/Census/library/publications/-2015/demo/p60-252.pdf

needed for a majority in the below median chamber for a net gain of 12% in representation for the group[22]. If only African Americans, Hispanics, and Native Americans are examined, they increase their margin of representation from 29.7% to 35.7% for a 20% gain in representation[23]. The proportional increase in representation goes up when Asians are excluded because their median wages are much higher than other minority groups. They still make considerable contributions to the overall proportion of minorities in the below median group and may be counted on when passing civil rights laws and labor rights.

It cannot be under-emphasized that the below median chamber is a coequal branch of government and has the opportunity to vote on all laws expected to pass the bicameral process. By dividing the population exactly in half, it effectively doubles the representational power of minorities when concentrated in only one part of the income-based electorate. The below median chamber can rely on government shutdowns, debt default threats, withholding tax breaks, and a whole host of other strategies to coerce economic reforms from the above median income chamber and the demographic majority. Threats are less effective than traditional negotiations; the below median chamber will regularly trade concessions to earn economic reforms that benefit them. The below median chamber has another advantage. It can rely on the middle class within the above median chamber to regularly support economic policies like progressive taxes, minimum wages, unionization rights, and reasonable property and labor rights.

---

[21] See appendix: Table 1

[22] See appendix: Table 1

[23] See appendix: Table 1

The majority demographic group doesn't benefit from the split in electorates because it previously maintained the implicit political power of majority demographic status. It would have had majority political power in the two parts of the bicameral legislature but will now be reduced to majority status in only the above median chamber. If there was no discrimination, then the majority demographic group would be equally represented in both the above median chamber and the below median chamber, and they would not have to make a concession to oppressed demographic minorities. Income based representation simply corrects these deficiencies in economy and representation. The over representation of a minority group in the below median chamber is temporary. Once it can leverage its political power to increase wages and build wealth in the community, the concentration of representational power will diffuse back into a more normally distributed population.

If one looks at population growth over the next 30 years, while holding the current wage discrimination constant, the margin needed for majority control of the below median chamber shrinks considerably every few years. In 2030, the Hispanic population grows to 18.9% of the overall population and nearly 21.4% of the below median population[24]. African Americans remain at 13.2% of the population with 16.8% of the below median chamber[25]. Native Americans shrink to just 0.8% of the

---

[24] Sandra Colby, and Jennifer Ortman. (March 2015). Projections of the size and Composition of the U.S. Populations: 2014 to 2060. P.88. U.S. Census Bureau. Retrieved from https://www.census.gov/content/dam/Census/library/publications/2015/demo/p25-1143.pdf

[25] Sandra Colby, and Jennifer Ortman. (March 2015). Projections of the size and Composition of the U.S. Populations: 2014 to 2060. P.88. U.S. Census Bureau. Retrieved from

overall population and 1% of the below median. Asian Americans grow to 6.6% of the population and nearly 4.6% of the below median chamber[26]. Combined, they will occupy 43.7% of the chamber with 83.6% of the majority needed to control the chamber, for a 10.4% improvement in overall representation[27].

By 2040, Hispanics will occupy 21.7% of the overall population and nearly 24.6% of the below median chamber[28]. African Americans will occupy 13.3% of the overall population and 16.9% of the below median chamber[29]. Asian Americans will grow to 7.4% of the population and more than 5.1% of the below median chamber while Native Americans continue to contribute 1%.[30] [31] In total, minority populations will occupy 44.5%

---

https://www.census.gov/content/dam/Census/library/publications/2015/demo/p25-1143.pdf

[26] Sandra Colby, and Jennifer Ortman. (March 2015). Projections of the size and Composition of the U.S. Populations: 2014 to 2060. P.88. U.S. Census Bureau. Retrieved from https://www.census.gov/content/dam/Census/library/publications/2015/demo/p25-1143.pdf

[27] See appendix: Table 2

[28] Sandra Colby, and Jennifer Ortman. (March 2015). Projections of the size and Composition of the U.S. Populations: 2014 to 2060. P.92. U.S. Census Bureau. Retrieved from https://www.census.gov/content/dam/Census/library/publications/2015/demo/p25-1143.pdf

[29] Sandra Colby, and Jennifer Ortman. (March 2015). Projections of the size and Composition of the U.S. Populations: 2014 to 2060. P.92. U.S. Census Bureau. Retrieved from https://www.census.gov/content/dam/Census/library/publications/2015/demo/p25-1143.pdf

[30] Sandra Colby, and Jennifer Ortman. (March 2015). Projections of the size and Composition of the U.S. Populations: 2014 to 2060. P.92. U.S. Census Bureau. Retrieved from https://www.census.gov/content/dam/Census/library/publications/2015/demo/p25-1143.pdf

[31] Sandra Colby, and Jennifer Ortman. (March 2015). Projections of the size and Composition of the U.S. Populations: 2014 to 2060. P.92. U.S. Census Bureau. Retrieved from https://www.census.gov/content/dam/Census/library/publications/2015/demo/p25-1143.pdf

pf the entire chamber, with 87.2% of the amount needed for a majority, and a 10% gain in overall representation compared with population[32]. At 87% of the seats needed for a majority, minority groups will have access to the bargaining power they need to protect their civil rights and economic interest. They could embargo budget negotiations and military appropriations until laws are presented that ensure they see less employment discrimination and wage discrimination. No laws will pass without their express consent.

These projections only account for the percentage of the population under $50,000 when in reality the figures should be adjusted upwards by the proportion falling under $53,657. These projects also don't disambiguate between voting age and non-voting age or eligible voters and non-eligible voters. These projections are just estimates. However, the projections of 2045 as majority-minority don't tease out this difference either. Econometric representation provides a 5-year advantage over waiting for the demographics to produce majorities. Five years is an awfully long time while the nation languishes under threats stemming from the expected loss of majority political power. There is one more significant difference. The econometric systems of representation split majority power between two chambers while demographic majority power may be both chambers. Splitting the power between two chambers may go a long way to prevent conflict between demographic groups during a shift in majority status. Majority power comes earlier for the minority demographic group but it stays with the majority demographic for many more years in environments of wealth inequality.

---

[32] See appendix: Table 4

The estimates don't consider one other important element. There is no effective way to price in the support for Caucasians who may ally themselves with an anti-discrimination and pro-equity party. The current estimate for when the U.S. becomes majority-minority is in 2045 while adjusted figures for econometric representation place majority control of the below median chamber closer to 2040[33] [34]. If Caucasians remain the majority-demographic group in the United States until 2045 and even a small portion of whites can deliver majority control for allied minorities in the below median chamber. Far earlier, possibly 2035. If minority groups can capture majority control over one part of a bicameral legislature nearly 10 years earlier than expected, they could fend off threats of debt defaults, government shutdowns, mass incarceration, and voter suppression efforts.

Women represent 48% of the U.S. work force and often receive wages at roughly 80% those of men[35] [36]. Women of all ethnicities can expect to capture majority power in the chamber. Identity politics will finally be supported by political power. For as long as there is economic discrimination in wage assignment and employment women and minorities will have implicit political control over one half of the bicameral legislative process. They will be over-represented in the below

---

[33] William Frey (March 2018). "The US will become 'minority-white' in 2045". Brookings. Retrieved from https://www.brookings.edu/blog/the-avenue/2018/03/14/the-us-will-become-minority-white-in-2045-census-projects/

[34] See appendix: Table 6

[35] Jared Bernstein, "Minimum wage: Who makes it?" *New York Times.* Last modified June 9th 2014. https://www.nytimes.com/2014/06/10/upshot/minimum-wage.html

[36] Elise Gould et al, "What is the gender pay gap and is it real," *Economic Policy Institute, last modified* October 20th, 2016. https://www.epi.org/publication/what-is-the-gender-pay-gap-and-is-it-real/

median chamber and have monopoly control over the chamber. These communities will elect their own representatives, staff oversight committees, and present legislation to be ratified by the other chamber.

The below median chamber will provide significant political advantages to women, minorities, the poor, and young adults but the above median chamber may also include dual income families which might have different attitudes despite having above median incomes. Nearly 59% of all families are dual income and a large portion of this demographic has two partners each making below median household wages[37] [38]. If the median family income is only $79,956 and both partners are working, then there is a large number of families where the two workers each make less than the median household income of $53,889[39]. Together they may make an above median household income, but they won't adopt an above median wage earners ideology. Policies that raise the wages of below median wage earners likely have a positive effect on the individuals in a dual income family above the average family income (when averaged with single income families. Higher minimum wage laws set prevailing wages that may affect them, higher union participation will increase the prevailing wage and benefit them, and progressive taxes on the 4th income quartile should coerce higher wages around the median.

---

[37] Jane Bianchi, "4 Dual-income households tell all: How we save and spend," Forbes, last modified Nov 4, 2013.
https://www.forbes.com/sites/learnvest/2013/11/04/4-dual-income-households-tell-all-how-we-save-and-spend/#4cc55f5b3e08

[38] "Dual income now most common / census bureau finds more women, even new mothers, joining workforce", *SFgate.com*, last modified Oct 24, 2000.
https://www.sfgate.com/news/article/Dual-Income-Families-Now-Most-Common-Census-2732395.php

[39] "Factfinder," U.S. Census, accessed on March 22nd, 2018.
https://factfinder.census.gov/faces/tableservices/jsf/pages/productview.xhtml?src=CF

However, political architects should expect mixed outcomes. In many respects, dual income families share sympathies with the above median income earners despite each partner making less than the median household income. Families with two incomes share the same costs in housing, food, and transportation. This gives them a higher standard of living compared to families with single incomes. The increased disposable incomes (savings) and accumulated wealth will afford more security than single individuals with access to one income and higher costs. Dual income families may resemble above median income earners in sympathies despite their inclusion in the below median electorate. This may be an appropriate compromise considering the split into below median and above median chamber shifts the median voter downward. A more comprehensive electorate based on median income would have a much higher value changing the political preferences of the median voter. This will be one of the more competitive demographic groups in the electorate.

The progressive nature of income-based representation can't be understated for economies with inherent discrepancies and discrimination within wage distributions or wealth inequality. Most nations have long histories of oppression and exploitation. Many were authoritarian, relying on Monarchs to make all public policy decisions. Others were aristocratic slave states, or apartheid democracies. Most nations regularly oppressed women regardless of wealth status or family status. These long histories are perpetuated today through culture. Laws remain unenforced and sanctions ineffective. Even if rights currently exist, the propensity for exploitative policies remains. It is based on precedent. And attitude. A median partition reverses this tendency. It corrects for the natural advantages a demographic majority has and provides minorities and women a more equal footing in the political markets.

Wage exploitation isn't restricted to minorities alone. Incomes usually rise with age. In democracy this poses a conundrum. Incomes generally provide more representation in democracies and older generations will use that leverage to protect their economic interests. They can suppress wages to control labor costs. They can donate more to political parties. They prefer lower taxes due to a reduced fear of income loss or lack of access to healthcare and education. The older generation are far less vested in the future of the nation than those younger than them. It's a simple calculation of the number of years left in their life.

Millennials in the U.S. are paid almost 20% less than what the Baby Boomers were paid, with half the accumulated net wealth, despite higher rates of experience and education[40]. This is wage exploitation. Their parents were paid almost 20% more for no other reason than their parents formed unions, raised the minimum wage, and paid progressive taxes. The intervening variable is higher wages and more wealth accumulation. The older generation is simply protecting their personal economic self-interests at the expense of the younger generation, who are often different ethnicities or religions in contemporary democracies with more open immigration policies.

This impacts the electorate. Younger generations will have more motivation to homestead and change their environment with political control over education,

---

[40] Josh Boak and Carrie Antlfinger, "Millennials are falling behind their boomer parents," *Yahoo Finance,* last modified on Jan 13th, 2017. https://finance.yahoo.com/news/millennials-falling-behind-boomer-parents-080144745.html

healthcare, and retirement. They will counterbalance the uncertainty in their own lives, or their children's lives, with more progressive attitudes towards unions and government. Younger peoples are more idealist and more optimistic due primarily to the length of time in consideration. They will be strong allies of other demographic groups experiencing wage exploitation or discrimination. They will be aligned along the same financial incentives and similar experiences.

Younger generations will be far more likely to be included in the below median chamber and benefit from the advantage in representation. Those who make higher wages and thus dissimilar incentives, or experiences will be included in the above median income chamber. By separating the income distribution into equal parts, the political system can emphasize the perspective of a majority of minorities, women, and youth. It is this perspective that suffers the most from deficiencies in economy and public policy. Political infrastructure must accommodate for the lack of agency, the over emphasis of the professional class and owners class, and the institutional advantage of property and business owners and it can accomplish this through an income-based system of representation. The below median income chamber will provide a powerful check against the raw political power of the numerical majority which generally over represents the majority demographic group, property owners, and corporations.

Splitting the electorate into below median and above median income chambers will split younger voters from older voters. The average ages in the below median income chamber should be far lower than the average age of a combined chamber. Likewise, the average age of the above median chamber will be far higher than the average age of combined chamber. The average legislative output of the chamber will reflect this identity. Younger persons generally have much lower incomes than older persons who have had decades of wage inflation and career success. This is purposefully engineered. Younger populations tend to be more socially progressive and more concerned about the future of the economy. Their forecasts are over 40-60 years. Older persons are far more conservative. They are seeking to preserve their wealth and to slow down social change. Their forecasts are only 20-40 years. Separating the two demographic groups will help them form an identity more useful for negotiating process. When isolated, the more specialized electorate will focus exclusively on their economic interests and barter more effectively for concessions and compromises.

Older persons generally enjoy more political power as they have been working towards promotion and election for decades more than an activist in their 20s or 30s. Traditionally, this has resulted in more conservative laws and public policy. A median partition promotes more younger people to positions of power resulting in an increased advocacy for more progressive policies. As these politicians grow older and gain more experience, they may enter the above median chamber but by then they will have already inculcated to the culture of progressive economic policies. Even if their economic interests are now different, they will remember their prior preferences and be more willing to compromise on certain issues. This should moderate the legislative output of both chambers, resulting in public policies that benefit both classes and more demographic groups.

In the same respect minorities discriminated against gain representational advantages, the youth of the nation will find their numbers concentrated in the below median chamber. This will help them organize and use collective bargaining to improve wages and benefits. The middle aged and older will have much higher incomes than the youth and be more distributed among the two chambers. This is especially true when the youth organize together with discriminated minorities for improvements in economic conditions. The older and wealthier populations will be concentrated as well, but in most traditional democracies they already occupied the more prestigious roles and enjoyed superior political power. They will now have to negotiate directly with the youth and minority groups to preserve that power.

A legislature split by median income and age may appear to be divisive and susceptible to political obstruction, but the median voter will continue to dominate the electorate. The more segmented the electorate is the more potential there is for agreement with the other chamber. Two divergent homogenous population have very little chance of finding common ground. The more heterogenous the two chambers are, the more opportunity there is for agreement on the less controversial issues. The greatest diversity will be found in the middle class, with age and income intersected at the median values. It will be a cross section of young and old, employee and employer, and representative of all ethnicities and religious preferences.

Likewise, retired persons on pensions may only qualify for the below median income chamber while high performing young professionals may qualify for the above median chamber. This will interject more conservative voters into the below median and remove them from the above median income chamber. This diversifies the electoral outcomes and legislative output of both chambers, making them more competitive and increasing the odds that legislation passes both chambers. However, current economic conditions will continue to heavily influence electoral outputs and the culture of reform. The middle class will be activist in protecting their interests and a moderate force for the upper and lower bounds in the electorate (really rich and really poor).

Institutions with strong democratic institutions should see significant wage growth across generations. The older generation should improve economic outcomes for the younger generations. When the youth suffer significant wage losses, it is likely due to a shift from one demographic group to another. A growth in wealth inequality is a telltale signs that the majority demographic group is rejecting its future as a minority group is a focus on public policy that maximizes wealth inequality. Their political agendas will emphasis policies on mass incarceration, deregulation. and budget austerity measures. A deregulated finance sector increases the probability of a significant economic correction. Large deficits and high spending expose the nation to government shutdowns and threats of premature default during a crisis. Low wages and high taxes breeds mistrust of the government contribution to populist and secession movements. Not only do these preferences indicate an increased likelihood of armed conflict but it will increase their odds of success.

The consequences of conflict might be a massive correction in the political market after the enlisted and civilian casualties alter the expected trajectory of the demographic shift. An equivalent of deaths on both sides of the divide will be a lager proportional share of total population for the minority demographic group. Thus, the violence will benefit the majority demographic group by delaying the transfer of political power. If the conflict results in independence, they may pursue authoritarian political organizations that disenfranchise the minority groups participating in the demographic shift.

The best gauge to estimate the possibility of conflict is how the majority demographic group treats the minority demographic group and the poor. This is a reflection on their expectations for treatment after assuming the role of minority in the country. The more fear they have of reciprocated abuse, the greater the chance of violence during the transition. The longer the history of severe abuses, the more likely the population will result on similar strategies when in crisis. A longer history will result in a larger population that supports abusive policies to preserve their superior position.

A majority-demographic group is most dangerous when they pass anti-democratic measures like gerrymandering, private campaign finance, suspend term limits, relax anti-corruption laws, participate in voter suppression, or disenfranchise voters (mass incarceration or restricted electorates). Using these strategies, the majority demographic group can retain majority political power long after they transition to minority status. These threats are less obvious than outright violence but just as dangerous. The threat of conflict increases when the period is extended, and representational accuracy diminishes. The measures will gain more support by the majority public than if outright violence was used. This is the danger. They can accomplish their goal with aggressive nonviolent policies.

The majority of the public won't be able to empathize with the victimized minority party and tolerance for the anti-democratic measures will grow.

Usually, the majority demographic group is blind to the actions of its own members. They rationalize the motivations and deny the malicious intent. Worse, they recognize the inherent benefit to their own immediate families and ignore the deleterious behavior. Despite the terrible consequences of the anti-democratic measures being widely known, it is doubtful they will provoke a strong reaction from the public to undermine or overturn them. This is especially true of they are implemented slowly over the course of several years. The less frequent the insults, the less involved the public will be.

The people will become acclimated to the poor legislative output, deteriorating economic condition, representational efficiencies and settle for a flawed democracy. Without the urgency of an implicit conflict the public has trouble identifying and addressing the emergent matter. A slow depreciation of conditions dislocates the policy from its consequences, muting the response of the oppressed populations. The public's short memory can't disentangle current conditions from future conditions under that stress. The result will be a compromised political system with diminishing trust in the government and support for its policies. Eventually, an administration will falter, or elections will be suspended during some national emergency. Democracy will die of exhaustion.

The majority-demographic group can usually silence dissent through the conventional political process. They can classify information. They can quash investigations and challenge the veracity of information. They can deny minorities an opportunity to make speeches and add public comment. The majority demographic group also has significant advantages in enlistment and the overwhelming support of the military establishment. The majority demographic group typically monopolizes the management and leadership of institutions like the media and other corporate organizations that might otherwise resist the violent or authoritarian tendencies of the majority during a demographic shift. This makes a dangerous situation so much more terrifying.

Democratic nations with liberal immigration and naturalization policies can experience significant changes in demographics. This can and will lead to current majority demographic status ethnicities receding to minority party status ushering in a period of considerable political risk and uncertainty. There has never been a successful transfer of political power between one majority demographic group to another. History is rife with examples of demographic violence. Most have occurred within monarchies or totalitarian nations, but democracies are at more risk.

Political power isn't transferred to the new majority demographic group in a despotic nation. This means the political elite preserve their power and the owners class preserves their positions. In democracies, the majority demographic group has implicit political power and a demographic shift will result in a new political elite with new regulatory and tax schemes. These are the inputs that potentiate conflict and violence. It is the expectation of a loss of power and property that will provoke the current majority to pass anti-democratic policies and incite violence against the growing minority population.

Class based representation decouples implicit political power from majority demographic status. When the electorate is split by class, wealth is the primary driver of representation and policy. Fewer people will identify with the majority demographic group with sympathies in ethnicity or religious affiliation. Income based representation divides the majority demographic into two parts based on class. Instead of a looking at a single 60% demographic majority, it will be split unequally between the two chambers. The demographic group may retain 40% of the above median chamber but be reduced to just 20% in the below median chamber. This presents an opportunity for a large minority group or a coalition of minorities to acquire majority power in the below median income chamber and a more equal footing with the demographic majority. Plus, a divided majority wont necessary resort to tribalism during crises if they identify along class lines first. It will be easier to transition from one dominant demographic group to another when the focus is on class, incomes, and wealth.

A below median income chamber, with a larger concentration of minorities, women, and young adults interrupts the polarization process. It's most immediate and urgent effect is preserving a platform for the minority party to publicly engage the abuses or possibility of abuse by the majority. They will already be organized before the event occurs and can more quickly mobilize to neutralize the threat when it first starts. More importantly, the below median income chamber allows the minority party to prevent the dangerous concentration of military bases, assets, and enlisted in states that might be hostile during an event.

The below median chamber must authorize all troop deployments and ensure that an allied states national guard or militia cannot be relocated overseas to coerce political concessions or deny them the capacity to defend themselves in a compromised election. The below median chamber must voluntarily consent to all military appropriations, authorizations, or bills that might pose a threat during a prolonged demographic shift. Minorities won't have to rely on the goodwill and rationality of the majority demographic group.

This makes class-based representation far more secure over longer periods of time when the horizons on demographic change are 50 or 100 years off into the future. Constituents in demographic systems are notoriously xenophobic due to the fear of loss of majority political power, even if the immigration does not include a pathway to citizenship. They extrapolate a 3% advantage in birthrates over the entire 100-year period, greatly exaggerating the probability of losing majority political power. Few demographic predictions remain accurate across a 100-year period. This is especially true if there are other interventions. Reducing poverty and making healthcare accessible could reduce birth rates. A change in public policy could provoke large population to emigrate away form the nation. Changes in immigration policy might increase another demographic group's prevalence and change the odds of securing political majority. No prediction is accurate with a 100-year horizon.

However, this irrational fear of an impending loss of political power could provoke the majority demographic group to rely on voter suppression, mass incarceration, or mass murder to permanently alter the electorate. This is truer in societies with high wealth inequality and long histories of racial abuse. If the majority demographic has brutalized minorities in the past, they will assume those minority groups will exact revenge on them with the same policies. They will fear the same persecution and exploitation they are guilty of. Chances are that the majority demographic group will continue to pursue economic policies that preserve poverty or subsistence level economic conditions for the emergent minority groups, thus maximizing the probability birth rates are maximized. The longer the minority group is subjected to abuse, the more likely they will reciprocate. This cycle of violence can be stopped with adequate voter protections and civil liberties. However, this is often a struggle for most democracies.

Income based representation shifts focus away from demographics and back towards class which conveniently avoids this 100-year horizon. Income based representation splits the electorate in two equal parts regardless of the average wage or demographic breakdown of the population. This effectively obfuscates or conceals demographic distributions of power from the public's awareness. When wealth inequality is high, the median wage will sink, and a larger portion of the population will have wages lower than the average wage. This will make those populations more susceptible to economic reforms that redistribute wages back to the middle class (median class). This should help the nation avoid political instability from the two most likely causes of institutional violence; demographic shifts and prolonged wealth inequality.

4 CLASS DIVISIONS

Most senates an example of nominal variables for representational coefficients. "Nominal-level variables communicate differences between units of analysis on the characteristic being measure"[41]. Senates assign an arbitrary number of senators to all states equally. Senates are nominal as they assign an equal number of senators to each state regardless of the states characteristics with no rank in status. A senator from one state has as much political power as a senator from another state and thus no rank. For this reason, arbitrary representation is a worse option during nation building. In anything, arbitrary representation is a form of entropy or disorder, where the ranking is an inverse of proportional representation with smaller states holding the prime positions.

Demographic-based systems such as assemblies contain interval level variables. "Interval-level variables give the most precise measurements between units of analysis. An interval-level variable communicates exact difference between units of analysis"[42]. In demographic systems, a state receives proportional representation based on the number of residents. The larger the number

---

[41] Phillip Pollock III, *The Essentials of Political Analysis* (California: CQ Press, 2016), pg. 26

[42] Phillip Pollock III, *The Essentials of Political Analysis* (California: CQ Press, 2016), pg. 26

of residents the more numerous the representatives. Each state is separated into a number of districts where every eligible person has one vote to elect those persons. "Interval-level variables are considered the highest level of measurement because their values do everything that nominal and ordinal values to - they allow the researcher to place units of analysis into different categories, and they permit units to be ranked on the measurement - plus they gauge fine differences between the units of analysis"[43].

Representational coefficients measure the difference in units, such as residents, GDP, or tax liabilities. Using a median income is no different. After the median income is multiplied by population, it provides proportional representation within the political union. Each state will be in ratio with the other states according to those terms. The difference in the two factors communicates an exact difference between the units of analysis. A change in either factor will produce a change representation. This measurability will promote more experimentation in public policy with higher median incomes promoting more political power for the state.

Demographic based representation is interval in one respect and nominal in another. All of the districts are ranked similarly with no particular order. This is not true in class-based representation where the districts are ranked in an ordinal manner around the median income. Class based representation employs both interval level properties and ordinal properties. "An ordinal-level variable communicates relative differences between units of analysis. Ordinal variables have values that can be ranked"[44]. The median partition implicitly divides the

---

[43] Phillip Pollock III, *The Essentials of Political Analysis* (California: CQ Press, 2016), pg. 26

electorate into two equal parts, with one above median and one below median chamber. The two chambers impart a ranking in wealth, with the above median chamber clearly having a superior social position but the two populations maintain equivalent representational power. Neither acquires an advantage over the other making it ideal for use in democratic systems of representation.

A median partition is a higher order form of organization. The districts carry more useful information and should improve the quality of legislation and public policy. The median partition provides majority rule and universal suffrage while improving the order of the political process. It's simply a better system of democracy. They retain the interval-level properties of a representational coefficient but enhances it with an ordinal ranking of the electorate. Wealth can be evaluated and ranked in terms of value. Incomes can be ranked in order of magnitude. Higher incomes are ranked higher than lower incomes. Larger incomes result in more accumulated wealth and more economic influence.

The median partition has other properties make it a superior option to conventional demographic-based systems of representation. They naturally split the electorate into two equal parts. Bimodal institutions produce a maximum dispersion of political power between the two classes. "Dispersion is the spread of cases across its values"[45]. The number of representatives allocated to each chamber is equal acquiring this standard in dispersion. The separation into two equal parts is

---

[44] Phillip Pollock III, *The Essentials of Political Analysis* (California: CQ Press, 2016), pg. 26

[45] Phillip Pollock III, *The Essentials of Political Analysis* (California: CQ Press, 2016), pg. 26

intended to mitigate or cancel out the superior economic advantage of the above median electorate. Thus, a class-based division will impart greater role identity with the division of labor, while preserving the highest quality in democratic entitlements.

A median is a resistant measure of central tendency making it unfazed by any positive or negative skew in the electorate[46]. The entire population is split into two equal parts, hence the bimodal descriptor. This is an ideal characteristic for a representational system. There is no structural benefit from increased income for constituents. The median voter will still dominate the political discourse by virtue of occupying the middle two income quartiles. The median voter shares economic sympathies with each other while the 1st income quartile and the 4th income quartile will be adversarial in economic outcomes. However, median voters should have more sympathies with the 1st income quartile when the average income is ranked higher than the median income, producing a positive skew in the distribution. The 4th income quartile has outliers in income. These outcomes will be disproportionately farther from the median income than the difference in income between the poorest 1st income and the middle classed 2nd and 3rd income quartiles.

The poorest won't identify with the richest, if they are segregated into a separate but equal chamber in the legislature, and thus will pursue economic policies that benefit them. Normally, political ideology may not emphasize this marked difference in economic outcomes, but a below median income chamber will require its representatives to maintain an income equal to or less

---

[46] Phillip Pollock III, *The Essentials of Political Analysis* (California: CQ Press, 2016), pg. 37

than the median, aligning their economic interests with the 1st and 2nd income quartiles. Conventional democracies typically pay their legislators above average incomes reducing parity in economic condition. A federal legislator earning $174,000 a year suffers from a deficit of economic sympathies with the 50% of citizens earning less than $53,889 a year[47] [48]. The federal poverty rate in the United States is $12,228 for a single individual producing a difference of $160,140 with members of Congress[49]. The federal legislators make nearly 14x as much as those citizens living at the poverty level and nearly 12.7% of the nation qualifies as living in poverty[50].

It is obvious that the agent-principal relationship is violated by this huge gulf in earnings between citizens and their representatives. Those earning $174,000 a year don't have the same economic concerns as those earning just $53,889. They don't have the same quality of healthcare. They don't have the same quality of retirement. They eat different food and wear different clothes. They don't live in the same communities and don't value the same government institutions. The legislators may advocate for social insurance and other government programs, but they are rarely beneficiaries or recipients. If they don't benefit directly, they are less

---

[47] Ida A. Brudnick, "Salaries of members of congress: Recent actions and historical tables," Congressional Research Service, accessed April 4th, 2018.
http://library.clerk.house.gov/reference-files/114_20150106_Salary.pdf

[48] Income and poverty in the United States," U.S. Census, last modified Sept 12th, 2017
https://www.census.gov/library/publications/2017/demo/p60-259.html

[49] Income and poverty in the United States," U.S. Census, last modified Sept 12th, 2017
https://www.census.gov/library/publications/2017/demo/p60-259.html

[50] "Income and poverty in the United States," U.S. Census, last modified Sept 12th, 2017
https://www.census.gov/library/publications/2017/demo/p60-259.html

enthusiastic about creating those programs or protecting them.

Most below median persons have trouble saving for retirement and paying tuition for their children. They may wait years before a raise in the minimum wage. Many below median persons live paycheck to paycheck, with income insecurity and food insecurity. This is not true for those earing nearly 3x as much at $174,000 a year for one partner contribution[51]. Most representatives would pursue economic policies that improved their own personal or family finances. They don't recognize the economic fears and interest of those they represent. For a representative to be a good agent for their constituencies they must share economic interests and have similar incomes. They must live in the same communities and use the same government services.

When the incomes for legislators are set at the median wage, the difference in salaries shrink to just $41,195 between median wage earners and poverty level wage earners. There is absolutely zero difference between the legislator's pay and the median income earner's pay. The legislator will serve as a perfect agent for the principle because they serve their own economic interests as well. The legislators will pursue economic policies that raise their wages and improve the government benefits they rely on. They will live in the same neighborhoods, care about the same schools, and worry about the same crime. If the below median income legislator wants to earn a higher wage, they will have to raise the wages for all of the residents in their district or jurisdiction.

---

[51] Ida A. Brudnick, "Salaries of members of congress: Recent actions and historical tables," Congressional Research Service, accessed April 4th, 2018.
http://library.clerk.house.gov/reference-files/114_20150106_Salary.pdf

This changes the operational definition of democracy in micropolitical arrangements. The legislature is the primary instrument for determining durable economic policy and fiscal policy. A Congress split between median incomes is far more exacting than a legislature allocated between districts and jurisdictions. A median income value is closer to the actual output than an averaged value because it excludes the outliers, who although are few in number can dramatically change the political output of a legislature with campaign donations or other forms of lobby. The below median income chamber has one other significant advantage over the more traditional demographic chamber. The representatives in a below median chamber are limited to median incomes, thus implicitly aligning their interests more to the middle class. The middle class is found in both chambers creating a gradient of support towards the below median chamber. A median partition is a simply more effective means for measurement than a non-differentiated districts or jurisdictions.

Micropolitical median partitions divide the population into above median and below median components. This is an incredibly personal operation. Individuals and families are ranked as high-income earners or low-income earners. This will charge the political environment with tension between the classes. Regressive economic reforms will redistribute wealth away from the below median income electorate and bestow it on the above median income electorate. Progressive economic reforms do the opposite. They redistribute wealth away from the above median income electorate and give it to the below median income electorate. Every tax law passed will favor one electorate over the other. Every labor law and business regulation will be viewed in terms of class preferences. The role identity will maximize tensions between the class, in an attempt to improve the wealth equality and economic output of the state or nation.

Political output occurs in cycles. The environment will dictate the dominant political themes. A functional democracy will attempt to correct market failures with public policy to achieve more equality in opportunity and economic outcomes. When prosperity is achieved, the public becomes less vigilant and seek to exploit deficiencies in the tax code or regulatory scheme. Deregulation movements follow periods of substantial economic expansion and prosperity while labor movements typically follow periods of economic stagnation or depression. Circumstances will contribute significantly to the internal dialogue of the nation and the persuasion of their legislative output. When the middle class loses wages over a period, a larger portion of the middle class located in the above median income chamber will support the economic reforms of the below median chamber. There will be a higher probability that tax laws and compensation laws change to correct the deficit in economic outcomes.

A full 50% of the population qualifies as middle class. The middle class includes those in the 2nd quartile and the 3rd quartile. These are the two middle quartiles. In optimal conditions, the middle class still has far more economic sympathies with the poor (1st income quartile) than they do with the wealthiest (4th income quartile). The relationship grows much stronger during adverse or extreme economic conditions. Half of the above median income chamber will qualify as middle class and support the policies of the below median legislators. This has profound implications for the below median chamber when their elected officials provide the leadership needed to negotiate concessions between the two chambers. The legislators from the above median chamber will be pressured to accept the legislation offered by the below median chamber.

Contemporary legislatures fail in this respect. The federal legislators from the United States all earn incomes greater than 96.4% of the remaining population[52]. There is no class distinction so there is no role identity or division of labor. The legislators will prefer laws that benefit them and thus coerce the whole economy in favor of the 4th income quartile. The legislator's higher wage makes them far less susceptible to changing economic conditions like healthcare inflation, education inflation, and wage stagnation. They can patiently wait out periods of high inflation with a wage 3x that of the median wage earner. There is very little that aligns a contemporary legislator to the majority of their constituents, especially in political systems without proportional representation.

Micropolitical income-based representation is an individual-level unit of analysis. Each person is evaluated individually in terms of their individual or household income. Each household is allocated to either the above median or below median income chambers. Their inclusion in one group at the exclusion of the other is an incredibly personal experience. It helps define their attitudes, their beliefs, and their aspirations. This is direct contrast to macropolitical income-based representation. Macropolitical representation occurs on an aggregate-level unit of analysis by organizing persons into sets of districts or states.

---

[52] "Income Percentile Calculator for 2017 US data," *DQYDJ.com,* last modified Aug 13, 2018. https://dqydj.com/income-percentile-calculator/

Rather than allocating persons or households to adversarial electorates, entire districts or states are determined to be either above median or below median income. A district or state is far more diverse with persons from almost every income quintile. The aggregate level unit of analysis is less homogenous in their experiences and beliefs. More competitive elections should result from the increased diversity of each district or state. The decision to use individual units of analysis versus aggregate units could have a profound impact on the culture and color of the nation. The selection will shape how institutions, parties, and political ideologies are founded and promulgated. This may help the state or nation avoid class-based conflict during periods of exaggerated wealth inequality or political corruption.

Voters choose their own filing status. This means voters can choose which chambers they vote in by selecting a joint filing or separate filing and changing the adjusted gross income used to justify eligibility in either chamber. This only works in cases where one spouse would be eligible and the other ineligible if their incomes where not averaged together. Usually, a family failing jointly will add both partners incomes together and each argent will be apportioned exactly half the Adjusted Gross Income. If partners earn unequal amounts, one may qualify for above median while the other remains below median. This comes at a steep cost. Everything has a tradeoff. Couples filing jointly pay fewer taxes than those couples filing separately. This should discourage most couples from filing separately. Still, a small minority will seek to exploit the eligibility requirements by switching filing statuses in years they feel they can impact elections the most.

Although, this may be a small margin of citizens, even a group of 2% or 3% could sway the outcomes of more competitive elections. Strategy by median voters may counteract some of the deleterious effects of deregulated campaign finance. A person with voting discretion is a more powerful tool than campaign contributions by the wealthy and corporations. The median voter usually dictates electoral outcomes and there will be powerful inducements for median income households to take on higher tax liabilities to have more control over the elections in their districts. Don't forget, this privilege is only earned by families whose averaged incomes should put them in a different chamber than their individual eligibility. These will primarily be single income families or families with significant differences in spousal incomes. However, these individual AGI results are averaged with their prior combined AGI results. This ensures that participants must be willing to take on the extra tax liabilities for at least few years. These decisions are not permanent, but they are not fleeting.

Any state or nation that uses an averaged income for eligibility naturally limits this electoral strategy by reducing the effectiveness of switching filing statuses during election years. In order to take advantage of this property, a household will have to decide their filing status 4 years prior and accept the financial cost of higher taxes. Naturally, most households will forgo the possibility of deciding on which chamber they vote in for the tax savings. Still, a small portion of households will elect to file separately and forgo the tax savings in order to split their votes among the two chambers. This will primarily be single income families in the 4th income quartile, who can afford the extra taxes.

Only 63% of the population participates in the labor force[53]. This leaves nearly 37% of adults without incomes to determine their status in either they below mean or above mean chambers. Inserting zeros into the mean wage calculation will change the outcome. Most mean wages are calculated from non-zero income values. This excludes nearly 37% of the population. Although most of those not working are pensioners or have other forms of income, a significant portion are zero wage earners. Persons not included in the labor force are *not necessarily unemployed.* "This category includes retired persons, students, those taking care of children or other family members, and others who are neither working nor seeking work"[54].

The average wage takes into account the outlier values while zero values are "usually excluded". This will favor the wealthier citizens by decreasing the representational ratio between districts. Once the zero values are factored in the average will be significantly lower, regressing back to the median. If an unadjusted mean wage was used, one chamber would serve 70% of the population and the other population would Serve the wealthiest 30% of the population. It would be an aristocratic version of government, with the highest wage earners monopolizing an entire chamber of the legislature. The median wage corrects this inequity by excluding the numerical superiority of outliers. They may occur in significant numbers but the figures are reduced

---

[53] Jeff Cox, "Labor force increase is biggest since 2003 as many Americans finally get back to work," *CNBC.com,* last modified March 9th, 2018.
https://www.cnbc.com/2018/03/09/labor-force-increase-is-biggest-since-2003-as-many-americans-finally-get-back-to-work.html

[54] "Labor force statistics from the current population," *Bureau of Labor Statistics,* accessed April 10th, 2018.
https://www.bls.gov/cps/lfcharacteristics.htm#nlf

to a single instance on the range of calculation. The median wage does the same for zero entries. In an average zero entries may receive over emphasis but in a median wage calculation they are simply place holders (assuming most entries are not zeroes).

A new measurement must be developed for use in voter registration. Officials should work with the census and tax bureaus to collect information on median Household Adjusted Gross Incomes. The median value must be taken for the entire adult population so that when the AGI from married couples is split in half, the two persons are allocated to the correct chamber. Zero entries must be included in this calculation, so the results are not skewed with far more people located in the below median due to an artificially high median income. This calculation will include all pensions and social insurance like disability or investment income. All citizens of adult age can be required to enter a tax form regardless of zero income or low income. The data will then be complete, and a more accurate figure can be teased out.

It is more appropriate to use the median household income as it averages out all households including single income families, dual income families, and single households. For example, median married couple incomes in New Jersey are $106,656 while median household incomes are only $72,093[55]. If a married couple has an income of $106,656 and the couple files jointly, they will each have $53,328 in AGI and vote in the below median chamber. Both partners would be eligible to vote and run for office. However, if the married couple elects to file separate and it was a single

---

[55] "Median Income," U.S. Census, accessed March 10th, 2018.
https://www.census.gov/search-results.html?q=median+income&page=1&state-Geo=none&searchtype=web&cssp=SERP&search.x=0&search.y=0

income family, then one partner would acquire $106, 656 in AGI and vote in the above median chamber while the other acquires $0 AGI and votes in the below median chamber.

The spouse earning $0.00 income would be eligible for voting in the below median chamber. This individual could even run for office in the below median chamber if they chose to. The constituents of the below median chamber would be aware of her married status and might demonstrate some bias if they estimate the person to have a lifestyle dissimilar to theirs. The states could require both partners to publicize their tax records as a requirement before running for office. This would allow the electorate to make a decision with full information on class identity before casting a ballot in favor of a candidate.

The nonfamily households, or single individuals, earned an average of just $39,000 which makes the median income of $72,000 far more attractive to them. Non-married Families have a median wage of $90,757 suggesting that nearly half of the families would earn less than $72,000 and gain replacement income while in office or substantially improve their income. Married families with combined incomes below $72,000 will also be attracted to civil service, but one spouse will have to take temporary leave in order to comply with income eligibility standards or file separately. The representative's income automatically raises to the median figure requiring the partner to file separately or disqualify the candidate during the next election.

Income eligibility for office and for registration will equal the length of the term for the office. This will instill more consistency into the lives of constituents and representatives. Representatives may be able to delay eviction from their office while representatives can adapt their expectations before the change occurs. The most important property of the multi-year average is smoothing out an average so that citizens aren't forced to change representatives and institutions haphazardly every year due to fluctuating incomes and rigidly fixed eligibility. With a smoothed-out average there will be less oscillation between the two median chambers. Representative income eligibility is checked before every election but if their income exceeds the maximum allowance during the term, they will be allowed to complete their term.

The representatives will have access to the median wage for income earners which is higher than the median income for residents which is adjusted down with zero entries and single income families. The salary for representatives will be set by the median income of other wage earners in the district, not the median income value used to determine electoral eligibility. This is intended to provide a slight economic incentive for participating in government. Factoring in a large number of zero entries is necessary to manufacture an accurate electorate but it would unnecessarily suppress the wages of a representative. The higher median wage still produces the intended economic sympathies. Many of the constituents are on retirement pensions and don't have the same costs as non-pensioners.

All filing continues to be compared to the household income rather than independent income. A representative filing independently has their single income compared to the household income. This provides some flexibility in economic outcomes outside of the filing status but if voters know the candidate is filing independently the voters will be able to speculate on the additional income and discriminate against the representative. Filing jointly provides tax advantages lost to persons filing independently. This introduced a financial cost that is outside of electoral preference for better agency. Candidates filing jointly present more agency due to improved accuracy in evaluating household incomes. On the margins, constituents should prefer information symmetry over ambiguity and uncertainty in agency. The rate of filing jointly will act as a gauge on the health of the political system.

Needless to say, political candidates in the below median income chamber will have to publicly release their income tax reforms. This will allow constituents to evaluate their status as jointly filed or independently field and recognize if a significant portion of their income comes from investments like real estate or securities. All income is qualified, even those incomes not paid from employment. This restricts the wealthy from seeking office in the below median chamber of their investments produce incomes higher than the household median income.

All of the assets and incomes on candidate's balance sheets are subject to review and scrutiny protecting against overt acts of corruption and implied relationships. A class-based system of representation must be able to dispel most of these concerns. However, a spouse who files separately without any employer or ownership of income producing assets may continue to qualify despite their spouse exceeding the limits. These situations will be evaluated by constituencies and the class-based representation should prime the electorate to discriminate against these candidates. The uncertainty of class and lack of opacity in income origination will be hotly debated by the candidates and the public in every election.

Income eligibility constraints on the legislators may create the perception of two classes when districts are separated into above median and below median states. Half of the districts will be located in the below median chamber and their representatives will have salary constraints. Often, there will be a number of proximate states with similar median incomes and this will create a perception that those representatives and states are valued less. This is intended. The body politics should prefer the poorer districts and states to have representatives paid at a lower rate. These politicians will become better soldiers for economic reforms that improve wage growth in the below median income group. These politicians will be warier of regressive taxes and policies that deregulate labor and compensation laws. Often, it is the representatives from the poorer and more rural states that back austerity measures and regressive taxes to the detriment of their constituents. If they can be coerced back into support of progressive economic policies by virtue of their own economic interests, it will be easier to correct the cyclical inequities of a market economy.

Representatives will implicitly assume the interests of their constituents. Below median representatives will have median incomes while above median income representatives will have above median incomes. They will enjoy more role identity with their constituents. Laws proposed in the below median will have language geared directly for employee and consumer classes. They won't be confused with the owners class or investors class. When economic reforms are debated, they won't confuse interests with other income brackets. The accounting details will be spelled out in terms of exclusive benefit to the working class. Class based representation is less confusing for constituents, improving their ability to identify their interests and act on defending them.

Political parties will focus on the benefit to their constituents rather than generic economic principles. A political party would lose the interest of the median voters if it did not comport its rhetoric and agenda to the specific economic interests of the voting class. In traditional electorates, the poor citizens vote for the same party as the wealthy citizens and economic interests are confused between generic economic principles and rhetoric that does not necessary pertain to them. A political party repeated talking about tax breaks for the wealthy is expected to do far worse in the below median income group than a party that drills down on wage reforms, labor protections, and progressive taxes. Parties will bend to the curvature of the chamber and develop economic policies that benefit those constituents.

This highly specialized information will contribute to the bargaining power of the below median income group. The above median chamber will have to offer incentives and protections for the employee and consumer class in every bill offered. They below median group won't be beguiled or ensorcelled by the elite class using institutional language for their own benefit over lower income persons. More importantly, reforms that target middle class wage earners will be popular in both chambers. Nearly half of each electorate will qualify as middle class rather than poor or rich, resulting in a nature gradient towards higher wages, progressive taxes, and more family friendly benefits like FMLA, sick time, universal health, and access to higher education.

Traditional electorates suffer from the confused self-interests of the poor who vote in support of polices for the wealthy. Combined, the 1st and 2nd income quartiles represent half of the total voters and alter the definition of a conventional median voter. The electoral output will be far different when the median voter is synthesized from the 2nd and 3rd income quartiles. If the average income out the median voter in a combined 1st and 4th quartile is higher than the median income, the legislature may pursue more policies that preserve the wealth advantage of the above median income population. This could perpetuate more regressive tax policies, lower wages, fewer unions, and a deregulated economy. A more competitive economy is not more productive as the wealth can rent seek, profiteer, and otherwise exploit low wage earners or other vulnerable populations.

Corporations and investors are able to protect their interests through the public policy process through lobby and expertise. This creates a gradient towards policy that protects the superior economic positions of the owners class and investors class. Elitism is built into the legislative process of demographic based systems. It's a cultural defect of ambition and trust. The median partition interrupts this process by enfranchising the below median income group with role identity and class perspective. The institution will continue to rely on professional expertise, but it will be checked by a greater affinity with union groups, consumer groups, and special interest groups that more adequately reflect their constituent composition. This will result in more legislative inhibitions when discussing tax breaks for economic stimulus or deregulatory regimes in pollution or labor. The greater scrutiny will result in fairer laws and more equitable laws. The institution will be the most important check against class inequity in wages, wealth, and civil liberties.

5 REBELLION AND REVOLT

One of the most important features of income-based systems of representation is the focus on class. The electorate is split into the haves and have-nots, with half of the population voting in the below median income chamber and the other half voting in the above median income chamber. Within the bicameral process, proposed laws need to satisfy the demands of both chambers before ratification. This will require the haves to more directly negotiate with and offer the have-nots more concessions during the legislative process. This invites class tensions into the rhetoric of an adversarial political process.

Class based rhetoric has been a powerful motivator in politics. This is evidenced by the success of Communism throughout the 20th century. Communism is a terrible economic system and a worse political system, but large populations enthusiastically supported it. More rural, less educated, and poorer populations will identify with the language used and the arguments made. Support for regime change usually starts in the countryside, where there are fewer government institutions or oversight. The low population density contributes to asymmetric information exchanges and less information transaction producing less trust in governments and more susceptibility to populist movements.

Communism emboldened the poor and motivated them for rebellion in nations all across the world. Despite communism failing, much of its class-based rhetoric still applies. The description of class-based conflict and economic exploitation might describe conditions in both totalitarian regimes and underperforming democratic regimes. This provides opportunities for income-based representation to successfully convert despotic nations or formerly communist nations towards democratic regime values. Populations everywhere are still susceptible to arguments about wealth inequality, private government, and employer exploitation and discrimination. Where ever political corruption and wealth inequality exist, there will be an opportunity to convert a nation to democracy with the rhetoric and language of income-based representation.

The rhetoric of class struggles will continue to be a vector for regime change, but now it will contribute to the progressive arc of history. Communism called for the abolishing of class while income-based representation depends on role identity and role specialization to improve the legislative process. Communism depended on draconian economic reforms to improve economic production while income-based representation will continue to rely on technological innovation and free markets. Class tensions will continue to motivate the youth, the poor, and other vulnerable groups towards social and economic reforms. Income based representation simply provides a more secure environment for the classes to engage each other in the perpetual struggle for survival.

Despite Communism being a terrible economic system rife with political abuses and misery, it was an extremely successful movement. This can be attributed to rhetoric focused on wealth inequality and the satisfaction of basic needs. In early capitalist societies wealth was horded and the benefits of organized production were monopolized by a small minority. Most people suffered under poverty, famine, and disease. Communism purposefully used the language of the haves and have-nots to divide the population unevenly. There were many more have-nots than haves, creating the precipice of rebellion and revolt. The terrible wealth inequality was the motivation and their advantage in number provided their confidence. Although successful for a few decades, Communism was an unmitigated disaster.

Communism failed primarily because it was premised on centrally managed economy. However, economy was not the only deficiency. Communism requires an authoritarian government to preserve order and maintain control over the economic infrastructure. When the public organized to protest the lack of food or modern technology, they were ruthlessly put down. Communism entailed a surveillance state, where paranoia and violence reigned supreme. These properties are more like parameters. There is a running clock on how long the administration or system will last. The lack of high quality commodities and surplus food will provoke more frequent and more sever responses from the public. It will eventually run out of time and be replaced by another administration that can provide the excesses its elite classes or poor demand.

Communism and democracy are incompatible. If the people could vote, they would prefer freer markets. Centrally managed economy can't exist outside of authoritative administrations. If a nation has the due process to regulate themselves and tax themselves, they will organize themselves into a moderate economy with labor laws and progressive taxes. The electorate will split the economy into a private sector and public sector, providing itself both public goods and a competitive market. However, nations with inefficient due process will accumulate defects. The lack of labor reforms and adequate public goods will contribute to political instability. The electorate will be susceptible to propaganda and populism. The rhetoric of free markets will be twisted into deregulatory schemes and trickledown economics. The result will be more wealth inequality and political corruption in the form of private campaign finance and corporate personhood. Cults of personality will coalesce around industrialists and the threat of despotism will loom on the horizon.

Income based representation is a good vector for democracy. It exploits the same deficiencies found in market economy that made Communism such a compelling solution. Wealth inequality and political corruption are powerful arguments for regime change and the class-based rhetoric of income-based representation will act to invigorate and mobilize the disaffected public. Class warfare and open revolt may result if a regime does not immediately respond with economic reforms or political reforms towards democracy. Income based representation is the most productive outcome possible after a populist rebellion. It distributes universal suffrage and proportional representation within the context of class and reform. The two go hand in hand. The worse the wealth inequality and political corruption, the stronger the argument for income-based representation.

The ability to maintain democracy is dependent on the nation's ability to acquire economic security for its citizens. "The expected life of democracy in a country with per capita income under $1,000 is about eight years. Between $1,001 and $2,000, an average democracy can expect to endure 18 years. But above $6,000, democracy lasts forever"[56]. Democracies that can pass economic reforms and foster economic growth are far more likely to succeed as democracies. This makes Class based systems of representation superior to traditional democracies. The focus on class identity and self-interests will promote economic policies that create wealth and distribute it better. A class-based system of representation will help democratic nations overcome the per capita barriers to democratic longevity. The public policy considered will be aimed at building the middle class with reasonable reforms. All income quartiles will be represented making it far likelier that the electorate reject all of the most severe and radical of reforms protecting the nation from gross mismanagement.

Formerly communist nations present the best conditions for income-based representation. Their public identifies with the class-based rhetoric. Many have even participated with most the their most recent historical figures and cultural icons associated with class-based warfare. Class tensions are on the surface of these nations and a significant portion of the public will support arguments for reform predicated on class-based representation. As the formerly communist nations become wealthier, the difference in economic outcomes will be more pronounced. The rural communities will be envious of the urban middle class and may seek remedy through class based political reforms. More importantly, the urban middle class may be emboldened by their economic success and with more disposable incomes and leisure time, will be more easily organized for democratic reform.

---

[56] Adam Przeworski, "Minimalist Conception of Democracy: A Defense." *Democracy's Value,* edited by Shapiro, I. and Hacker-Cordon, C. *(*Cambridge: Cambridge University Press, 1999), pg. 16

However, there are far more under-performing and corrupt democracies in the world. These nations are the most susceptible to the class rhetoric of income-based representation. Nearly 3/4ths of all nations are considered to be democratic but only 25% are classified as democracies[57]. This means half of the nations in the world are considered low quality democracies. These flawed democracies are rife with wealth inequality, political corruption, and representational deficiencies. All are susceptible to regime change (or secession). This may be to the benefit of other nations who seek administrations with economic sympathies. This may be to the benefit of citizens and organizations within the nation, who are discriminated against or oppressed by the current regime. Class based representation provides a powerful inducement to change, with more productive outcomes. Rebellion and revolt are never the safest strategy, but it may still be the most effective.

Most successful rebellions are not populist revolts but rather movements organized by business owners and the most highly educated persons of a state. The impression that wealth-based representation benefits the owners class and investors class more than ordinary persons will result in more support for regime change or rebellion when those with more access to capital are more willing to loan it to a fledgling state. The wealthy will enjoy a significant presence in the above median chamber and benefit from the representational advantage of being concentrated in one chamber.

The top 20% of the income distribution will command 40% of the representation in the above median

---

[57] Economists Intelligence Unit, "Democracy Index 2017: free speech under attack," EIU.com, 2018. http://www.eiu.com/Handlers/WhitepaperHandler.ashx?fi=Democracy_In-dex_2017.pdf&mode=wp&campaignid=DemocracyIndex2017

chamber. There are many financial inducements for the professional classes and middle class to coordinate with the wealthiest 20%. The wealthy will be able to negotiate with and elicit cooperation from the middle class and professional classes making up the remainder. The bicameral process depends on cooperation from both chambers to pass laws. The wealthy could protect themselves by obstructing redistributive laws or regulations they believe to be too constrictive.

The wealthy will have to continue to govern by consensus as they will only have a 40% margin in the above median chamber. However. they will still have enough political power to quash most populist policies. If an aggressive form of socialism rooted in the below median chamber, it is predictable that a larger margin of the middle class would support their obstruction of gross redistribution of wealth or the abolition of property rights. There are no such guarantees in a conventional demographic legislature. If due process is entirely based on majority rule, then a populist movement could acquire a simple majority and make sweeping economic reforms. The 4th income quartile will prefer a political system that insulates them from populist movements originating in the 1st income quartile.

Populism is starved in a median partition split by class. The clarion call for wealth redistribution or more radical economic reforms will die in the below median chamber with little or no support in the above median chamber. The middle class will be stalwart protectors of property rights and government entitlements. They will resist radical redistribution by the bottom and the gross exploitation of the top. This is an optimal environment for businesses who depend on well-regulated labor and securities markets to provide stable market economies to profit from. If an economy is too profitable, it will become unequal and unstable. It is then susceptible to market corrections and other wealth disruptions. If deregulation produces too much wealth inequality, the middle class will support more restrictive policies and higher progressive taxes. Business will seek to preserve the highest profits possible for the longest period and this is made possible by a class-based system of representation with a median partition.

If wealth-based systems of representation attract more support from corporations and local businesses, it will increase its odds of achieving a durable state of democracy. Modern corporations have access to an almost unlimited amount of labor and capital and the wealth can leverage these resources for regime change. The wealthy have tremendous political power at their disposal and are already deeply entrenched within the bureaucracy of government. If they feel as though this method for political organization benefits them, they will support it even if the motivation originates from within the lower classes or median class. Both classes benefit from the higher organization involved in a median partition, and thus have incentives to mobilize for regime change. Let them see what they want from the rhetoric. In this respect, it is a mirror of the culture and a reflection of the nation's economic and cultural histories.

There are identifiable policies and strategies that a party can pursue to maximize their chances at secession or regime change. Regime change can be used to overthrow an authoritarian administration or replace a flawed democracy with another republican government. It might take years or decades to fully implement, but most measures should already be priced into due process. Although only some parties may pursue these policies to counteract the systemic risk of corruption or authoritarianism, they will find agreement with other parties that seek to exploit the risk during demographic shifts or periods of excessive wealth inequality. It will be an arms race, as parties weaponize public policy and build in multiple triggers for a conflict. The positions are interchangeable as their roles won't be defined until some future event or episode. Political instability can last a decade or two, with several elections intervening between the start and finish, making it impossible to predict the parties position or the timing of the event. Thus, both parties have to price in the possibility of occupying both the opposition party and the majority party

An opposition party that expects to lose power should first move to decouple the ability of the establishment party to print money during periods of economic duress. The best method is to relocate the printing press from a Treasury department to an institution outside that of elected government. A Central Bank is the optimal recipient if the private sector appoints a portion of the officers with the state executives of the primary political parties electing the rest. Switching the power to print money to an institution with mixed leadership will face less resistance during the transition while simultaneously introducing concealed and ambiguous outcomes during crises.

If 40% of the Central Bank's officers are appointed by private sector firms (commercial and investment banks) and the remaining 60% are appointed by prior executives, this could eliminate the federal government's ability to print money, after a default when borrowing isn't an option due to higher rates or seized markets. At the very least, it introduces uncertainty to the loyalty and reliability of an institution when there is strong support for an institutional protest by an opposition party. A currently elected administration might find itself as a minority on the board of governors of the central bank, if the private sector is split on support for the government, and if half of the prior political appointments support open revolt.

The opposition party should move to impose a debt ceiling on all borrowing. Deficit Financing is a conventional method of economic stimulus which under crisis conditions could result in a situation where the excessive accumulation of debt could provoke fear in the public, thus validating threats of default. The debt ceiling measure represents a second opportunity to have a budgetary crisis. This could effectively double the probability of default or event when it follows a standard budgetary process. An opposition party need only control one part of a bicameral process to impose a debt default on the nation and this can be timed for convenience. A split Congress or a Presidential Veto could trigger a default from failing to raise the debt ceiling.

A debt default could trigger an economic correction in the stock markets, bond markets, and sharply curtail consumption. If unemployment and foreclosures follow conditions like those preceding World War II can be recreated. The public would act erratically and support more radical parties and economic reforms. This is the perfect environment for a secession movement or regime change. A debt default in one year can have ramifications in the years that follow making them less afraid of the electoral consequences. Many political parties might expect more support on the local and state level after they cause a default. This is especially true if a government is succumbing to authoritarianism and the democratic process is threatened with corruption or obstruction.

Budgets must be passed every year or two and a prolonged government shutdown is an effective way to eliminate a government. There may not be enough emergency funding measures available to an administration to persist through a government shutdown that last more than just a few weeks. This is especially true if the government shutdown is followed by a debt default, but a standalone shutdown could cripple the public sector and ruin the economy. The two measures working in tandem will deny the current government tax revenue while deny it deficit financing through official channels and unofficial channels when borrow rates skyrocket. There are a large number of consequences to a government shut down and debt default. All aid an opposition party intending to prosecute a rebellion.

The next most effective strategy a nation can employ is a Tax Holiday. Governors can redirect corporate and individual tax revenues from the federal government back to the state or local governments. They can do this by penalizing the behavior on the state level. Sanctions can range from monetary penalties to jail time and prison. Corporations are typically responsible for paying the majority of payroll and income taxes and if they can be discouraged from remitting funds back to federal government, the federal government can be denied nearly half their expected revenues from income taxes and corporate taxes. If an opposition party is seeking open revolt, they will want the support of corporations. Fines and other penalties, such as confiscation, could increase the number of compliant companies. This is especially true if the corporations suspect the rebellion will be successful.

Not only could this redirect 50% of federal income taxes to confederate states but it would deny the federal government nearly 50% of their federal income tax and payroll revenues. In a worst-case scenario, the debt default would double the borrowing costs of the government in an environment where the government has access to only 50% of its peace time funding. In the event of a war, federal expenditures would increase 150% placing incredible strains on a finance system that can't borrow and doesn't have a legitimate budget. This will exacerbate if stock exchanges and credit market seize in reaction. The use of debt defaults, government shutdowns, and structured tax holidays could effectively disable a nations ability to marshal its resources or raise an army to defend itself.

National Guards are military units that come from specific states or regions. They are also typically under dual control of the states and the federal government. This suggests that a Governor could call up their National Guard as a means to provoke rebellion or prevent secession. If all of the enlisted come from the same state, they are far more likely support the public regardless of which political party controls the federal government. They will certainly take up arms if their communities are aggressively put down during protests or threatened by another state or coalition of states.

Opaque or concealed National Guard deployment procedures contributes to the likelihood of an event. Not only can the rotation of National Guard armies be structured to deny one political party access to those assets during a crisis, but their fair use will increase the odds of conflict and the probability of successful secession. A single rotation of National Guard armies might represent just 5% of the total standing army but it could be equal to 20% of the total national guard armies apportioned to the opposition party. This could cripple a party's ability to prevent an authoritarian usurpation or secession. This risk is maximized if the lopsided deployment occurs in a Presidential election year, especially if prior election years were contested and future ones might be compromised.

National Guard armies like those in the United States represent 50% of front line combat troops[58]. If the opposition party challenges, they could quickly call to arms nearly 25% of all front-line combat troops available to the nation. This also denies the federal forces nearly 25% of their standing army. The threat of secession increases if the national guard armies have veteran experience. This gives the leadership more confidence of success and that can be a dangerous ingredient if debt default and shutdowns are already practiced public policy. Although lacking support structures of the federal army, the national guard units would still have the support of local communities and states. There they can find locally sourced food, shelter, civil employees, munitions, and everything else a militia needs to operate an extended campaign. Nearly 75% of an army is dedicated to support roles and rebel states can easily substitute local resources during an emergency.

More importantly, the state national guards can be quickly integrated with local police forces. Anti-Drug policies can to contribute to the militarization of police force. Police departments are often composed of veteran combatants with access to military hardware and training and who are subject to local or state rule. In the United States, the police force of 1 million is almost equivalent in number to the standing army of 1 million[59]. A standing

---

[58] "About the national guard," nationalguard.mil, accessed on April 20th, 2018. http://www.nationalguard.mil/About-the-Guard/Army-National-Guard/

[59] "2016 Index of U.S. Military," *Heritage.org*, accessed on April 20th, 2018.

army may only be 25% frontline combat troops with 75% in supporting roles.

In reality, police acting as militia represent nearly 4x as many combatants as the standing army, prior to any adjustments from national guard armies. Police forces can be homogenous populations, resistant to any demographic changes that are present in the civilian population. The police regularly participate in anti-protest policies, which happen regardless of whether it occurs in a democratic country or despotic one. This could be a serious weakness in an environment of both organized protest and disorganized riot in event of a debt default, prolonged government shutdown, or a challenge.

Debt defaults and government shutdowns will contribute to the defection of Standing army if a viable alternative is presented. If the opposition party can shut down the government or cause a default, it can prevent monthly salaries to be paid to enlisted. Enlisted without pay are much more likely to defect to states or confederate nations that can pay their wages. This will bolster the numbers of those who would have confidence without the inducement. It will disincentive continued enlistment in the federal army for those who might otherwise support the establishment regime. Confederate National Guards can expect to acquire nearly 25% of the standing army from the onset, and defection rates could increase this to more than 30-40% if the majority party isn't careful. Many insurrections and civil wars were fought with smaller margins of support in the armed services.

Gun cultures will produce more terrorism and the individual acts of radicals could provoke conflict between the states. A farmer protesting grazing fees with armed resistance could find popular support in the community and stymie the federal government's ability to manage their properties. Militia members might reject interference from any federal law enforcement agencies monitoring them. Anti-government sentiments in the public could coalesce into a rallying call for confederates threatening secession or independence. Random acts of violence could proliferate through the state and result in larger mobilizations like rallies and protests. Other demographic groups might retaliate and create conditions for mob justice or riots. Strong gun cultures bolstered by weak regulations could create tinderbox conditions that might elicit a reaction by the Governor which may include activating the National Guard armies.

One of the more effective policies for a political party considering revolt or secession to pursue is the privatization of the military. By shifting active deployments from enlisted to mercenaries, the opposition party can deny the army veteran troops during a conflict. Many of the veteran troops will have allegiances to corporate boards and oligarchs rather than the federal government. This increases the systemic risk of conflict as mercenaries would just as willingly support an uprising as a usurpation attempt. Politicians who expect to lead a secession or hostile takeover will want to ensure they have an option to purchase a private army if the opportunity to use one arises.

More mature nations with nuclear arsenals are at more risk of successful secession. The debt defaults and government shutdowns increase the risk of defection in Submarine Commanders, Squadron commanders, or Silo commanders. If even one nuclear platform defects it could effectively end a conflict despite overwhelming force aligned against the secessionist states. This is a force multiplier that makes even a modest defection rate of 10-25% an incredible potent threat. Nations with thousands of nuclear weapons actually face the greatest probability of defection. It is much more likely a majority party concede to secession under the threat of nuclear war.

Obstruction of the legislative process by an opposition party is intended to maximize the number of disaffected citizens and a poor regulatory environment. Obstructing the government prevents economic reforms like raising the minimum wage to reduce poverty, increasing taxes to lower the deficit, and regulating too big to fail companies. Poverty and exacerbated wealth inequality will contribute to the large number of disaffected and distrustful constituents ready to support a challenger. Fewer financial regulations result in more volatile market movements and more disruptions with worse consequences. If a government can't respond to a market correction with regulation, it increases the probability of occurring again. The minority party can exploit every opportunity that arises when government expenditures increase and the deficit balloons. Maintaining these conditions is a huge benefit to an opposition party contemplating insurrection.

Opposition parties can pursue economic policies and populist rhetoric that makes the public more susceptible to insurgency or resistance. A culture emphasizing gun rights is one predictor of future conflict. Small arms generally aren't effective in rebellions, but they can complement National Guard armies, the homogenous police forces, and defectors from the standing army. An establishment party will have to dedicate resources to hold cities or rural communities when they should otherwise be allocated to front lines or other duties. The most dangerous threat a gun culture poses is in the threat of a pogrom against a vulnerable population or minority population that can permanently alter the composition of an electorate in a democratic country. Even if the insurrection or rebellion fails, it could produce irrevocable and permanent damage to another population and alter the course of the country. Wars bring with them lawlessness, especially in rebel states, and law enforcement may never have the opportunity or the resources to investigate all of the populist abuses.

Opposition parties should continue to support anti-tax policies in order to maximize the wealth of the private sector. The wealth inequality will contribute to a culture where magnates and industrialist have the resources necessary to contemplate insurrection and then carry it out. The owners class will accumulate political power and then aggressively protect it. There are fewer consequences for the wealthy and they won't fear public criticism. This makes them far more likely to support authoritarian policies. The more wealth they accumulate, the more risk there is in electoral cycles that could produce candidates favoring higher minimum wages, progressive income taxes, and estates taxes.

The more effective the owners class is at suppressing wages, the larger the share taxes are of disposable income, and the more they will resist forms of taxation. The more the government attempts to lower taxes to reduce the burden, the more debt it accumulates and the worse the outcomes are for citizens. Not only do these tax policies frame an adversarial relationship between the public and the government, it actually Increases the rate of debt accumulation and provides opportunities for future default and challenge. Periods of excessive austerity can erode effectiveness of law enforcement trying to prevent the organization or mobilization of an insurgency or rebellion.

Rhetoric about less government, smaller government, and deregulation breeds disdain and distrust of government. It sets a trend towards less effective government with less authority. The less the government taxes and regulates, the more resistant the citizenry will become to taxation and regulation. Business is organized around a system of feudalism with owners having near despotic control in the same respect a monarch would. Corporate boards resemble the lords or fiefs prevent in aristocratic classes. This role produces similar identities and ideologies and set the owners class on an adversarial position to that of democratically elected officials.

Revolutions often start years or decades prior to their implementation. It is a cultural phenomenon that is expressed across generations. It springs from ambition, expectations, and experience. This is truer in democratic nations who grant the rebellious population tremendous political power. They can obstruct government to maximize participation. They can diminish its quality of democratic entitlements with gerrymandering or unrestrained campaign finance. They can pursue austerity measures to weaken the government and make it susceptible to debt defaults and government shutdowns. They can also pursue regressive taxes to stoke the anti-government sentiments in the electorate.

In most respects, democratic government are far more susceptible than communist or despotic regimes that don't require legislatures to support budgets, or don't have debt ceiling measures, and elections that can be compromised. Democracy is voluntary. It depends on trust, respect, and duty. All of these principles can be broken by a single generation that no longer supports democratic elections or fears the consequences of disobedience. The people of a democratic nation should be wary of political parties that pursue the same policies described in this book. It is often excused as negligence, short sightedness, or greed but nobody can argue against the consequences of the policies. The people must be articulate in their defense of democracy, and organize into political parties willing to risk everything to preserve their freedom and voting rights. In order to do this, they must be able to recognize the unintended or undisclosed effects of the policies previously described. They must be effective in rallying the common cause against these policies and parties.

There is a slippery slope to these tactics. They are far more favorable to the party or administration that prefers despotic outcomes. It is harder for parties that want to preserve democracy to use these strategies to counteract authoritarian policies in a current administration. The authoritarian will simply allow the democratic infrastructure to melt away and in replace it with their figurehead. However, these strategies will make it clear to the nation the intent or ambition of the regime. These policies are declarations by a minority party in rebellion against a regime with creeping despotic tendencies. They should be effective enough to disrupt the economy and to interrupt government revenues. More importantly, they will force the state governments and local governments to make a stand for liberty and democracy.

There is one condition that maximize systemic risk of conflict in a democracy. Demographic shifts are the most dangerous period in the lifecycle of a democracy. There is a loss of implicit political power when one demographic majority is replaced by another. Not only does this make one political party or coalition predisposed to secede from the union while they are in the minority, but it makes it more likely they pass anti-democratic measures and restrict voting rights to preserve their power despite the change in majority demographic status.

The probability of demographic violence is higher when the majority demographic group prefers public policy focused on mass incarceration and regressive economic policies. This demographic group regularly oppresses and abuses minorities and will therefore fear abuse while a minority themselves. They will immediately reference their own behavior and tendencies and project them on the new majority demographic group. This will exacerbate the urgency with which the current majority demographic group protects their current position. Demographic shifts are highly predictable and are broadcast far in the future. This lends ample opportunity for one party to prepare to secede or pursue a more authoritarian government.

The second most dangerous condition is explicit wealth inequality and political corruption. The lack of adequate housing and food insecurity is a compelling motivator for organizing against a government. Democracy should reduce the probability of an event by legislating its way out of danger. In a functioning democracy, the median voter dictates most political outcomes and when an economy shifts towards poverty and opportunity deficits, the party focusing on compensation and tax reforming benefiting the middle class should win more elections and relieve the economic stress on the below median income group.

In democracies suffering under abusive filibuster cultures with low quality democratic entitlements, the necessary economic reforms are not passed and there is a significantly greater chance of rebellion or revolt. Peasants have always organized into mobs to demand recourse. Today, the threat is much greater with the speed of information flows from 24-hour news networks and the internet. Populations can mobilize more quickly in response to an event making the state or nation more unstable. Worse, unqualified opinions and incorrect information tends to circulate faster than verified facts, creating a tendency towards worse outcomes.

Democratic nations undergoing demographic shifts often accumulate massive wealth inequality as the majority group passes laws intended to preserve their wealth and political power. Risk of conflict is maximized when both presents are present, and this rarely produces productive economic or voter reforms. Rebellions often result in autocratic regimes regardless of the democratic intentions of the participants. Democracy represents an uncertainty in outcome that war time leaders inherently distrust. They will often seek to delay elections or diminish the authority of deliberative bodies while embroiled in conflict. Those currently in power will want to preserve it at all costs and those that gain power will want to keep it. The best strategy to protect democratic voting entitlements is through patience and incremental reforms. It may entail varying degrees of exploitation, oppression, and suffering but strategic non-violent resistance and a fully informed electorate are the surest ways to ensure due process and democracy survives in an environment of demographic shifts and wealth inequality.

Bibliography

"2016 Index of U.S. Military," Heritage.org, https://index.heritage.-
    org/-military/2016//us-military-power/us-army/

"About the national guard," nationalguard.mil, accessed on April
    20th, 2018.http://www.nationalguard. mil/About-the-
    Guard/Army-National-Guard/

Bernstein, Jared. "Minimum wage: Who makes it?" *New York Times.*
    Last modified June 9th 2014. https://www.nytimes . com/20-
    14/06/10/upshot /minimum- wage.html

Bianchi, Jane. "4 Dual-income households tell all: How we save
    and spend," Forbes. Nov 4, 2013. https://www.forbes.Com
    /sites/learnvest/2013/11/04/4-dual- income-households-tell-
    all-how-we- save-and-spend/#4cc55f5b3e -08

Boak, Josh, and Antlfinger, Carrie. "Millennials are falling
    behind their boomer parents," *Yahoo Finance,* Jan 13th,
    2017. https://finance.-yahoo.com/ news/millennials-falling-
    behind-boomer-parents-080144745.html

Brudnick, Ida. "Salaries of members of congress: Recent actions and
    historical tables. "*Congressional Research Service.* Feb 23rd,
    2016. http://library. clerk.house.gov/referencefiles/114_ 2015-
    0106_Salary.pdf

Colby, S. L., and Ortman, J.M. (March 2015). Projections of the size
    and Composition of the U.S. Populations: 2014 to 2060. P.9.
    U.S. Census Bureau. Retrieved from
    https://www.census.gov/content/-
    dam/Census/library/publications/2015/demo/p25-1143.pdf

Cox, Jeff "Labor force increase is biggest since 2003 as many
    Americans finally get back to work," *CNBC.com,* March 9th,
    2018. https://www.cnbc.com/2018/03/09/ labor- force-
    increase-is-biggest-since-2003-as-many-americans-fin-ally-get-
    back-to-work.html

"Dual income now most common / census bureau finds more
women,
    even new mothers, joining workforce", *SFgate.com,* Oct 24,

2000. https://www.sfgate.com/-news/article/Dual-Income-Families-Now-Most-Common- Census-2732395.php

DeNavas-Walt, Carmen, and Proctor, Bernadette (September, 2015). Income and Poverty in the United States: 2014. P.14. U.S. Census Bureau. Retrieved from https://www.census.gov/content/dam/-Census/-library/publications/-2015/demo/p60-252.pdf

Economists Intelligence Unit, "Democracy Index 2017: free speech under attack," EIU.com, 2018. http://www.eiu.com/Handlers/WhitepaperHandler. ashx? fi=Democracy_ Index_2-017.pdf&mode=wp&campaigned=DemocracyIndex2017

"Factfinder," U.S. Census, accessed on March 22nd, 2018. Retrieved from https://factfinder.census.gov/faces/tableservices/jsf/ pages/productview.xhtml?src=CF

Frey, William (March 2018). "The US will become 'minority-white' in 2045". Brookings. Retrieved from https://www.brookings.edu-/blog/the-avenue/2018/03/14/the-us-will-become-minority-white-in-2045-census-projects/

Gould, Elise, Schieder, Jessica, Geier, Kathleen. "What is the gender pay gap and is it real," *Economic Policy Institute,* October 20th, 2016. https://www.epi.org/-publication/what -is-the-gender-pay-gap-and-is-it-real/

"Income and poverty in the United States." U.S. Census." Sept 12th,2017. https://www.census.gov/ library/publications/ 2017/demo/p60-259.html

"Income Percentile Calculator for 2017 US data," DQYDJ.com, https://dqydj.com/income-percentile-calculator/

Kurtzleben, Danielle. "Let them eat cake," *U.S. News.* Jan 9th, 2014. https://www.us-news.com/news/blogs /data-mine/2014/01/09/let-them-eat-cake-members -of-congress-14-times-more-wealthy-than-average-american

"Labor force statistics from the current population," *Bureau of Labor Statistics*, accessed April 10th, 2018. https://www.bls.gov-/cps/lfcharacteristics.htm#nlf

"Median Income," U.S. Census, accessed March 10th, 2018.https:/-/www.census.gov/-searchresults.html?q= median+in-come&-page=1&stateGeo=none&searchtype =web&cssp=SERP-&search.x=0&search.y=0

Plumer, Brad. "Who doesn't pay taxes, in eight charts," *The Washington Post*, Sept 18, 2012. https://www.washington-post.com/news/wonk/wp/2012/09/18/who-doesnt-pay-taxes- incharts/?noredirect=on&utm_term=.d3989 fade602

Pollock III, Phillip. *The Essentials of Political Analysis.* California: CQ Press, 2016.

Przeworski, Adam. "Minimalist Conception of Democracy: A Defense.*" Democracy's Value,* edited by Shapiro, I. and Hacker-Cordon, C. Cambridge: Cambridge University Press, 1999.

"Quick Facts," U.S. Census, accessed March 20th, 2018 https://www.census.gov/-quickfacts/fact/table/US/PST045217

Weisinger, Jordan. *The Fountain; nation building with econometric representation.* South Carolina: CreateSpace, 2018

Weisinger, Jordan. *Class Struggles*. South Carolina: Kindle Direct, 2018

Weisinger, Jordan. *Market Democracy.* South Carolina: Kindle Direct, 2019

Weisinger, Jordan. *The Fury; Class Struggles and Income-based Representation.* South Carolina: Kindle Direct, 2019

Footnotes

Jordan Weisinger, Market Democracy (South Carolina: Kindle Direct, 2019).

[2] Jordan Weisinger, The Fountain; Nation building with econometric representation (South Carolina: Create Space, 2018).

[3] Jordan Weisinger, The Ferry: Resistance and rebellion with tax-based representation (South Carolina: Kindle Direct, 2019)

[4] "Median Income," U.S. Census, accessed March 10th, 2018. https://www.census.gov/searchresults.html?q=median+income&page=1&stateGeo=none&searchtype=web&cssp=SERP&search.x=0&search.y=0

[5] Danielle Kurtzleben, "Let them eat cake," U.S. News. Last modified Jan 9th, 2014. Https://www.usnews.com/news/blogs/data-mine/2014/01/09/let-them-eat-cake-members-of-congress-14-times-more-wealthy-than-average-american

[6] "Median Income," U.S. Census, accessed March 10th, 2018. https://www.census.gov/search-results.html?q=median+income&pa-ge=1&state-Geo=none&searchtype=web&cssp=SERP&sea-rch.x=0&search.y=0

[7] "Median Income," U.S. Census, accessed March 10th, 2018. https://www.census.gov/searchresults.html?q=median+income&page=1&state-Geo=none&searchtype=web&cssp=SERP&search.x=0&se-arch.y=0

[8] Brad Plumer, "Who doesn't pay taxes, in eight charts," *The Washington Post*, last modified Sept 18, 2012. Retrieved from https://www.washingtonpost.com/news/-wonk/wp/2012/09/18/-who-doesnt-pay-taxes-incharts/?noredirect=on-&utm_term=.d3989fade602

[9] DeNavas-Walt, Carmen, and Proctor, Bernadette (September, 2015). Income and Poverty in the United States: 2014. P.14. U.S. Census Bureau. Retrieved from

https://www.census.gov/content/dam/Census/-library/-publications/-2015/demo/p60-252.pdf

[10] DeNavas-Walt, Carmen, and Proctor, Bernadette (September, 2015). Income and Poverty in the United States: 2014. P.14. U.S. Census Bureau. Retrieved from https://www.census.gov/content/dam/Census/-library/publications/-2015/demo/p60-252.pdf

[11] DeNavas-Walt, Carmen, and Proctor, Bernadette (September, 2015). Income and Poverty in the United States: 2014. P.14. U.S. Census Bureau.Retrieved from https://www.census.gov/content/dam/Census/-library/publications/-2015/demo/p60-252.pdf

[12] Colby, S. L., and Ortman, J.M. (March 2015). Projections of the size and Composition of the U.S. Populations: 2014 to 2060. P.9. U.S. Census Bureau. Retrieved from https://www.census.gov/-content/dam/Census/library/publications/2015/demo/p25-1143.pdf

[13] DeNavas-Walt, Carmen, and Proctor, Bernadette (September, 2015). Income and Poverty in the United States: 2014. P.14. U.S. Census Bureau. Retrieved from https://www.census.gov/content/dam/Census/-library/publications/-2015/demo/p60-252.pdf

[14] Colby, S. L., and Ortman, J.M. (March 2015). Projections of the size and Composition of the U.S. Populations: 2014 to 2060. P.9. U.S. Census Bureau. Retrieved from https://www.census.gov/content/dam/-Census/library/publications/2015/demo/p25-1143.pdf

[15] DeNavas-Walt, Carmen, and Proctor, Bernadette (September, 2015). Income and Poverty in the United States: 2014. P.14. U.S. Census Bureau.Retrieved from https://www.census.gov/content/dam/Cen-sus/library/publications/2015/demo/p60-252.pdf

[16] DeNavas-Walt, Carmen, and Proctor, Bernadette (September, 2015). Income and Poverty in the United States: 2014. P.17. U.S. Census Bureau. Retrieved from

https://www.census.gov/content/dam/C-ensus/library/publications/-2015/demo/p60-252.pdf

[17] DeNavas-Walt, Carmen, and Proctor, Bernadette (September, 2015). Income and Poverty in the United States: 2014. P.34. U.S. Census Bureau. Retrieved from https://www.census.gov/content/dam/Census/library/-publications/-2015/demo/p60-252.pdf

[18] Colby, S. L., and Ortman, J.M. (March 2015). Projections of the size and Composition of the U.S. Populations: 2014 to 2060. P.9. U.S. Census Bureau. Retrieved from https://www.census.gov/content/dam/Census/library/publications/2015/demo/p25-1143.pdf

[19] Colby, S. L., and Ortman, J.M. (March 2015). Projections of the size and Composition of the U.S. Populations: 2014 to 2060. P.9. U.S. Census Bureau. Retrieved from https://www.census.gov/content/d-am/Census/library/publications/2015/demo/p25-1143.pdf

[20] DeNavas-Walt, Carmen, and Proctor, Bernadette (September, 2015). Income and Poverty in the United States: 2014. P.36. U.S. Census Bureau. Retrieved from https://www.census.gov/content/dam/Census/-library/publications/-2015/demo/p60-252.pdf

[21] DeNavas-Walt, Carmen, and Proctor, Bernadette (September, 2015). Income and Poverty in the United States: 2014. P.14. U.S. Census Bureau. Retrieved from https://www.census.gov/content/dam/Cen-sus/library/publications/-2015/demo/p60-252.pdf

[22] See appendix: Table 1

[23] See appendix: Table 1

[24] See appendix: Table 1

[25] Colby, S. L., and Ortman, J.M. (March 2015). Projections of the size and Composition of the U.S. Populations: 2014 to 2060. P.88. U.S. Census Bureau. Retrieved from https://www.census.gov/-content/dam/Cen-sus/library/publications/2015/demo/p25-1143.pdf

26 Colby, S. L., and Ortman, J.M. (March 2015). Projections of the size and Composition of the U.S. Populations: 2014 to 2060. P.88. U.S. Census Bureau. Retrieved from https://www.census.gov/content/dam/Census/library/publications/2015/demo/p25-1143.pdf

27 Colby, S. L., and Ortman, J.M. (March 2015). Projections of the size and Composition of the U.S. Populations: 2014 to 2060. P.88. U.S. Census Bureau. Retrieved from https://www.census.gov/content/dam/Census/library/publications/2015/demo/p25-1143.pdf

28 See appendix: Table 2

29 Colby, S. L., and Ortman, J.M. (March 2015). Projections of the size and Composition of the U.S. Populations: 2014 to 2060. P.92. U.S. Census Bureau. Retrieved from https://www.census.gov/content/dam/Census/library/publications/2015/demo/p25-1143.pdf

30 Colby, S. L., and Ortman, J.M. (March 2015). Projections of the size and Composition of the U.S. Populations: 2014 to 2060. P.92. U.S. Census Bureau. Retrieved from https://www.census.gov/content/dam/Census/library/publications/2015/demo/p25-1143.pdf

31 Colby, S. L., and Ortman, J.M. (March 2015). Projections of the size and Composition of the U.S. Populations: 2014 to 2060. P.92. U.S. Census Bureau. Retrieved from https://www.census.gov/content/dam/Census/library/publications/2015/demo/p25-1143.pdf

32 Colby, S. L., and Ortman, J.M. (March 2015). Projections of the size and Composition of the U.S. Populations: 2014 to 2060. P.92. U.S. Census Bureau. Retrieved from https://www.census.gov/content/dam/Census/library/publications/2015/demo/p25-1143.pdf

33 See appendix: Table 4

34 William Frey (March 2018). "The US will become 'minority-white' in 2045". Brookings. Retrieved from https://www.brookings.edu/blog/the-avenue/2018/03/14/the-us-will-become-minority-white-in-2045-census-projects/

35 See appendix: Table 6

36 Jared Bernstein, "Minimum wage: Who makes it?" *New York Times*. Last modified June 9th 2014. https://www.nytimes.com/2014/06/-10/upshot/minimum-wage.html

37 Elise Gould et al, "What is the gender pay gap and is it real," *Economic Policy Institute, last modified* October 20th, 2016. https://w-ww.epi.org/publication/what-is-the-gender-pay-gap-and-is-it-real/

38 Jane Bianchi, "4 Dual-income households tell all: How we save and spend," Forbes, last modified Nov 4, 2013. https://www.forbes.com/-sites/learnvest/2013/11/04/4-dual-income-households-tell-all-how-we-save-and-spend/#4cc55f5b3e08

39 "Dual income now most common / census bureau finds more women, even new mothers, joining workforce", *SFgate.com*, last modified Oct 24, 2000. Https://www.sfgate.com/news/art-icle/Dual-Income-Families-Now-Most-Common-Census-2732395.php

40 "Factfinder," U.S. Census, accessed on March 22nd, 2018. https://factfinder.census.gov/faces/tableservices/jsf/pages/productvie w.xhtml?src=CF

41 Josh Boak and Carrie Antlfinger, "Millennials are falling behind their boomer parents," *Yahoo Finance,* last modified on Jan 13th, 2017. https://finance.yahoo.-com/news/millennials-falling-behind-boomer-parents-080144745.html

42 Phillip Pollock III, *The Essentials of Political Analysis* (California: CQ Press, 2016), pg. 26

43 Phillip Pollock III, *The Essentials of Political Analysis* (California: CQ Press, 2016), pg. 26

44 Phillip Pollock III, *The Essentials of Political Analysis* (California: CQ Press, 2016), pg. 26

45 Phillip Pollock III, *The Essentials of Political Analysis* (California: CQ Press, 2016), pg. 26

46 Phillip Pollock III, *The Essentials of Political Analysis* (California: CQ Press, 2016), pg. 26

47 Phillip Pollock III, *The Essentials of Political Analysis* (California: CQ Press, 2016), pg. 37

48 Ida A. Brudnick, "Salaries of members of congress: Recent actions and historical tables," Congressional Research Service, accessed April 4th, 2018. http://library.cl-erk.house.gov/reference-files/114_20150106_Salary.pdf

49 Income and poverty in the United States," U.S. Census, last modified Sept 12th, 2017. Https://www.census.gov/library/publications/2017/d-emo/p60-259.html

50 Income and poverty in the United States," U.S. Census, last modified Sept 12th, 2017. Https://www.census.gov/library/publications/2017/d-emo/p60-259.html

51 "Income and poverty in the United States," U.S. Census, last modified Sept 12th, 2017. Https://www.census.gov/library/-publications/2017/demo/p60-259.html

52 Ida A. Brudnick, "Salaries of members of congress: Recent actions and historical tables," Congressional Research Service, accessed April 4th, 2018. http://library.clerk.h-ouse.gov/reference-files/114_20150106_Salary.pdf

53 "Income Percentile Calculator for 2017 US data," *DQYDJ.com,* last modified Aug 13, 2018. https://dqydj.com/income-percentile-calculator/

54 Jeff Cox, "Labor force increase is biggest since 2003 as many Americans finally get back to work," *CNBC.com,* last modified March 9th, 2018. https://www.cn-bc.com/2018/03/09/labor-force-increase-is-biggest-since-2003-as-many-americans-finally-get-back-to-work.html

[55] "Labor force statistics from the current population," *Bureau of Labor Statistics*, accessed April 10th, 2018. https://www.bls.gov/cps/lf-characteristics.htm#nlf

[56] "Median Income," U.S. Census, accessed March 10th, 2018. https://www.census.gov/search-results.html?q=median+income&page=1&state-Geo=none&searchtype=web&cssp=SE-RP&search.x=0&search.y=0

[57] Adam Przeworski, "Minimalist Conception of Democracy: A Defense." *Democracy's Value,* edited by Shapiro, I. and Hacker-Cordon, C. (Cambridge: Cambridge University Press, 1999), pg. 16

[58] Economists Intelligence Unit, "Democracy Index 2017: free speech under attack," EIU.com, 2018. http://www.eiu.com/Handlers/White-paperHandler.ashx?fi=Democracy_Index_2017.pdf&mode=wp&campaignid=DemocracyIndex2017

[59]"About the national guard," nationalguard.mil, accessed on April 20th, 2018. Http://www.nationalguard.mil/About-the-Guard/Army-Nat-ional-Guard/

[60] "2016 Index of U.S. Military," *Heritage.org*, accessed on April 20th, 2018. Https://index.heritage.org/military/2016/assessments-/us-military-power/us-army/

Index

Table 1: 2014 Race and Income for Below Median Chamber

Race	% of population Under 50k (quintiles)	% of population	% of below median	% change in representation
Caucasian	44.0%	62.5%	55.0%	88%
Hispanic	56.6%	15.3%	17.3%	13%
African American	63.7%	13.2%	16.8%	27%
Asian under	34.5%	5.4%	3.7%	69%
Native American	63.7%	1.2%	1.5%	27%
Sum		35.1%	39.4%	112%

Table 2: 2030 Race and Income for Below Median Chamber

Race	Proportion of populati	Proportion of po	% of below median	% change in representation
Hispanic	56.6%	18.9%	21.4%	13%
Black	63.7%	13.1%	16.7%	27%
Native American	63.7%	0.8%	1.0%	27%
Asian	34.5%	6.6%	4.6%	-31%
Sum		39.4%	43.7%	111%

Table 3: 2035 Race and Income for Below Median Chamber

Race	Proportion of populati	Proportion of po	% of below median	% change in representation
Hispanic under	56.6%	20.2%	22.9%	13%
Black	63.7%	13.2%	16.8%	27%
Native American	63.7%	0.8%	1.0%	27%
Asian under	34.5%	7.0%	4.8%	-31%
Sum		41.2%	45.5%	111%

Table 4: 2040 Race and Income for Below Median Chamber

Race	% of population Under 50k (quintiles)	% of population	% of below median	% change in representation
Hispanic under	56.6%	21.7%	24.6%	113%
Black	63.7%	13.3%	16.9%	127%
Native American	63.7%	0.8%	1.0%	27%
Asian under	34.5%	7.4%	5.1%	-31%
Sum		43.2%	47.6%	110%

Table 5: 2045 Race and Income for Below Median Chamber

Race	% of population Under 50k (quintiles)	% of population	% of below median	% change in representation
Hispanic under	56.6%	23.0%	26.0%	113%
Black	63.7%	13.4%	17.1%	127%
Native American	63.7%	0.8%	1.0%	27%
Asian under	34.5%	7.8%	5.4%	-31%
Sum		45.0%	49.5%	110%

ABOUT THE AUTHOR

Jordan David Weisinger graduated from the Johns Hopkins University with a M.S. in Data Analytics and Policy (2019), Northwestern University with a M.A. in Public Policy and Administration (2017), and the University of Massachusetts Amherst with a M.B.A in General Management (2015). His undergraduate degree is in Literature from the University of Delaware (2000) where he focused on literature from the Gilded Age in the United States. Jordan has written several books detailing how alternate forms of democracy can be used for nation building,

He focuses on high-quality systems that deliver anti-discriminatory and anti-corruption properties, improving their long-term viability and interest from special interest groups. He has written about GDP-based systems (2017), Income-based systems (2018), Tax-based systems (2018), and Asset-based systems (2020) and intends to continue exploring how econometric systems of representation can improve outcomes for nation building efforts. Recently he has written books focusing on non-violent strategies executives and legislators can use to resist authoritarian movements or successfully wage a war for independence. Strategic Non-violent Institutional Protests are intended to make it more likely that the econometric systems of representation described in earlier books are used for nation building in wars of succession, secession, or democratization.

www.ingramcontent.com/pod-product-compliance
Lightning Source LLC
Chambersburg PA
CBHW031229250726

48655CB00005B/1864